# WAR
In The Heavenlies

# AND

# PEACE
In Your Life

A Woman's Guide to
# War in the Heavenlies
# And Peace in Your Life
Coral Kennedy

With a Foreword by Ruthanne Jacobs

and Dr. Lawrence Kennedy

FAME Publishing, Inc.
Irving, Texas

FAME Publishing, Inc.
5215 North O'Connor Boulevard, Suite 200
Irving, Texas 75039

© 1991 by Coral Kennedy
All rights reserved. Published 1991
Printed in the United States of America

98 97 96 95 94 93 92 91   5 4 3 2 1

Unless otherwise indicated, all Scripture quotations are taken from the King James Version of *The Holy Bible*.

Scripture quotations marked (AMP) are taken from *The Amplified Bible*. Old Testament copyright © 1965, 1987 by The Zondervan Corporation. *The Amplified New Testament* copyright 1958, 1987 by The Lockman Foundation. Used by permission.

Scripture quotations marked (NASB) are taken from the *New American Standard Bible*, © 1960, 1962, 1963, 1968, 1971, 1972, 1973, 1975, 1977 by The Lockman Foundation. Used by permission.

Scripture quotations marked (NIV) are taken from the *HOLY BIBLE, NEW INTERNATIONAL VERSION*. Copyright © 1973, 1978, 1984 International Bible Society. Used by permission of Zondervan Bible Publishers. All rights reserved.

Scripture quotations marked (NKJV) are taken from *The New King James Version*. Copyright © 1979, 1980, 1982, Thomas Nelson Inc., Publishers.

Scripture quotations marked (Phillips) are taken from *THE NEW TESTAMENT IN MODERN ENGLISH*, Revised Edition by J.B. Phillips. Copyright © 1958, 1960 and 1972 by J.B. Phillips. Reprinted with permission of Macmillian Publishing Company.

Verses marked (TLB) are taken from *The Living Bible* © 1971. Used by permission of Tyndale House Publishers, Inc., Wheaton, IL 60189. All rights reserved.

Photo credit: cover — Lauren Shaw

ISBN 1-880563-00-2

*For we are not fighting against people
made of flesh and blood,
but against persons without bodies —
the evil rulers of the unseen world,
those mighty satanic beings and
great evil princes of darkness
who rule this world;
and against huge numbers of wicked spirits
in the spirit world.*

Ephesians 6:12 (TLB)

# Contents

Foreword .................................... ix
Preface ..................................... xi
Acknowledgments ............................ xvi

### Part I
### What Is Spiritual Warfare?

Introduction ................................. 3
1 Know that a Woman's Place Is in Armor ....... 9
2 Master "Spiritual Warfare 101" ............... 17

### Part II
### What Are Your Enemy's Capabilities?

3 Give No Place to the Enemy of Your Soul ...... 31
4 Recognize the Battlefield ..................... 41
5 Identify Your Enemy's Weapons .............. 49
6 Break the Chains of Strongholds .............. 59

### Part III
### What Are Your Capabilities?

7 Unleash the Supernatural Strength of Your Forces. 73
8 Pick up Your Weapons of Power .............. 83
9 Overcome by the Power of the Spirit .......... 103

### Part IV
### Women: To Arms!

10 Fight until You Win ......................... 123

### Part V
### Appendixes

Appendix A  Receive God's *Personal* Word for You! 139
Appendix B  Declare Your Proclamation of Power . 143
Appendix C  Pray the Word of God .............. 147

# Foreword

When I was first asked to write a foreword for this book, I didn't hesitate because I count the author as one of my dearest friends and would do anything to support her. Having since read the manuscript, I feel compelled to write for another reason.

Coral has been given a Word from God — a Word directed to the '90s woman; a working Word — a usable Word. This is a Word that enlightens the reader's mind to the *whats* and *whys* of the confusing days that we live in and shows how to effectively deal with problems facing women of the '90s.

This is a must-read book for every pastor's wife as well as every lay woman. It is rightly called a handbook, for I am sure that whoever buys it will refer to it time and time again.

Ruthanne Jacobs

I have lived with this woman of God for 14 years. I know the statements in this book are true. These principles will totally revolutionize your life.

Lawrence Kennedy

# Preface

It was in Korea that God gave me a mandate to share this message with you.

A month after two alarming spiritual experiences, my husband, Lawrence, and I were invited to Korea by Dick Bernal, a member of Dr. Paul Yonggi Cho's Church Growth Board. After prayerful consideration, Lawrence and I felt impressed to accept Dick Bernal's gracious invitation to go pray and study at Dr. Cho's church in Korea. Lawrence felt something unusual in his spirit and said, ''Coral, I feel this trip is more for *you* than for me.''

''Okay,'' I said, ''I receive that.'' (I had heard that the shopping was good in Korea, but seriously doubted that was what God meant!) Our congregation generously donated the funds to pay our way—much to my dismay. (It is difficult to receive such a gift!) We flew to Korea to learn about church growth and to pray.

One day about halfway through the trip, I was sitting in a pastors' workshop, listening to a gifted teacher's excellent message. So far nothing very unusual had happened—except a few good deals on purses and luggage! (Again, I knew that was not why God had called us to Korea.)

Suddenly, I heard the Lord speak in my spirit, ''Teach the women how to do spiritual warfare.''

I immediately replied, ''Me? Certainly there are others much more qualified. Are You *sure* You want *me*, Lord?''

Then, before I knew it, something very powerful happened. As fast as I could, I started writing down what I heard the Lord strongly speaking in my spirit. He was giving me Scripture after Scripture to teach you how to do spiritual warfare.

In speaking for more than 11 years to women's groups and at different conferences, I have received many inspired messages from the Lord; but this is the most sovereign, divine move that has ever taken place in my life. I was excited, because whenever the Lord moves sovereignly like this, something good is going to happen.

While we were still in Korea, God confirmed His Word to me through a great man of God. Later that night after the Lord gave me all these verses on spiritual warfare, we were invited to dinner. Lawrence and I thought we would be eating with our good friends, Dick and Carla Bernal.

However, C. Peter Wagner and his wife, Doris, also joined us. He is a missionary, educator, author, theologian, and world renown authority on church growth. Doris is an authority on spiritual warfare, and has taught in several South American countries. We had never met this couple before, but quickly made friends and began to talk about the Lord over dinner.

For no apparent reason in the natural, Peter turned and said, ''Tell me, Lawrence and Coral, what do you know about spiritual warfare?''

Suddenly, I felt cornered by the Lord, but I shared a few of our experiences. Then I explained what had happened to me in August of 1989. It was a life-threatening encounter with a demonic entity that I believe was the death angel. I felt compelled to repeat several times to Peter and Doris that I am not one who sees demons in doorknobs everywhere I go!

*Preface*

After I told this story, Peter looked at Doris, knowing what she was about to say. "Coral, do you realize," Doris asked, "that you just described *exactly* what I saw in my room less than a year ago?" Doris, too, had encountered the demonic entity!

Then Peter explained that earlier in the week, Dr. Cho had described a similar experience that he had last year. Peter and Doris told us that the pastor of the largest Spirit-filled church in South America had also experienced an encounter with the death angel. I realized that I was not alone and felt a bit more at ease about discussing this unique experience. (I will share it in the upcoming pages of this book.)

This was only the beginning of the revelation that the Lord was to drop into my heart about the severity of our spiritual warfare. Soon, I had more than enough material to fill a three-session seminar and a book on spiritual warfare for women. Since that time, I have received speaking invitations to teach women how to destroy the works of the devil in their lives. This was further confirmation of the Word God had spoken to me in Korea.

I am not one who promotes myself to be continually in front of people, speaking. Instead, I have made a habit of exhorting and encouraging others to launch out to fulfill the call of God upon their lives. Believe me, I have plenty to say; it is not that I am at a loss for words. I merely know that the members of the Body of Christ have God-ordained ministries and calls upon their lives — and that includes *you*! This is why I promote other women. However, God apparently had another plan in mind this time. He wanted *me* to teach this message. Together as we study His Word in this book, we are going to see miracles happen in *YOUR LIFE* — in Jesus' Name!

## What Can You Expect?

We all have areas in which the enemy is manipulating us to some degree. I am ready to see those chains and shackles fall off women's lives so we can glorify God in everything we do.

Through this book, I believe God is going to bring you into a new kind of freedom, restoration, and victory in every area of your life — body, soul (mind and emotions), and spirit.

This is not a wishy-washy, namby-pamby book for women, but intensive training on spiritual war! Because this is an *advanced course*, I will not address basic Christian doctrines such as: why the devil exists; how he fell from heaven; or why God sent His Son, Jesus, to redeem mankind from sin. If you need help in these areas, please feel free to write me. Our church has material to instruct you in these areas. (See also Appendix A.)

I want you to understand more than anything else in this book, that you truly are in a life-and-death battle for your life and for everyone you influence. However, God gave His Word to you to teach you how to overcome. I am dedicated to helping you learn what God has for you so you can *conquer* the enemy of your soul.

The Bible says that we are not to be ignorant of the enemy's devices (II Corinthians 2:11). After reading this book, you will not be ignorant any longer. You will know when and how the enemy is attacking you, and how to overcome him.

I want to declare that throughout this book, my intention is never to glorify *anything* or *anyone* but *Jesus Christ*. Remember that He is more powerful than the devil and his demons. You do not have to fear anything if you are in Christ.

*Preface*

Let's go to the Lord now and ask that His will be done.

Dear Lord,

    We give You this time that we have together right now. I ask that You give this precious woman ears to hear the voice of Your Spirit, speaking to her.

    Let Your will be done in my life and in the life of each woman who will ever read this book in Jesus' Name. We praise You now. Amen.

I have been praying that the Lord would guide women, who need this message, to read this book. You are an answer to prayer! Now as you read these pages, listen for the voice of the Holy Spirit, guiding you into all truth.

# Acknowledgments

To my husband, Lawrence,
who encouraged me to write this book;
to our congregation
for diligently engaging in spiritual warfare
for our city, the nation and the world;
to Kay Leeper for all of her assistance
in the preparation of this book;
to our dear friends —
Larry and Melva Lea,
Dick and Carla Bernal, and
John and Ruthanne Jacobs —
without their love, support, and divine input in my life,
this book could not have been completed

# Part I
# What Is Spiritual Warfare?

# Introduction

SUDDENLY, WE HEARD A DEEP MALE VOICE echoing through our bedroom. It was a hot Saturday night in August just before midnight. My husband, Lawrence, and I had just lain down in bed after travelling all day from a conference in Arizona.

I had not told Lawrence what had happened the night before in our hotel room at the conference; but I was beginning to wonder if I should have explained it in detail. It was the most frightening experience I had ever had in my entire life.

My mind was racing. Was this voice we were now hearing somehow related to the tremendous fear I had felt the night before? There was no time to explain it all to Lawrence now. First we had to deal with this voice in our bedroom.

Stunned, Lawrence and I instantly and simultaneously sat up in bed together and looked at each other in shock. We had just heard my name spoken audibly in our bedroom, although we could see no one there.

Instinctively, I said, "Honey, go check the front door."

"We don't ever use that door," Lawrence replied. "Why should I check it?"

"*Please* check the front door!" I pleaded again. It seemed quite urgent to me.

Lawrence had just heard my name called out loud in our bedroom by an "invisible voice," so he decided it might be wise to do what I had asked! When he went to the front door and checked it, he was shocked to find it unlocked! Normally, we enter our house from the garage and have very little occasion to use the front door. However, we had just arrived home from being gone for about a week; apparently a friend had come in to check on things and had forgotten to lock the door.

In our neighborhood at that time, many children were being abducted from their homes within a one-mile radius of where we lived, and now we found our front door unlocked!

Although Lawrence had recognized the voice in our bedroom that night, he suddenly had some serious questions for me. "Honey," he asked, "why did the Lord call out your name? Why did He let *me* hear it?" Lawrence suspected that I knew something he didn't, and he was right!

I had to tell him about what had happened to me the night before. Yes, I was sure now that this was somehow related to the events of the prior evening.

THE NIGHT BEFORE the Lord spoke my name audibly in our bedroom, Lawrence and I had been supporting John and Ruthanne Jacobs in a Forceful Men's conference that they were hosting in Phoenix, Arizona.

This was shortly after God had commissioned us, under the direction of Dr. Larry Lea, to begin Church on the Rock-North in Dallas. We were experiencing great growth and were very busy. In the natural, it did not appear to be a good time to take off for a conference in Phoenix; but I really

*Introduction*

felt impressed to go, and we wanted to support John and Ruthanne in any way we could.

I had no idea that I was about to face death — the most frightening experience of my life. It would radically change me forever.

After the last meeting of the conference, Lawrence and I went to bed, exhausted. Although he fell asleep quickly and was sleeping very soundly, I was completely awake (as I usually am the moment my head hits the pillow — no matter how tired I might be when I first lie down). I began praising God for all the great and exciting things that had happened at this conference.

I was wide awake — when suddenly ''it'' entered our room! My peripheral vision caught something in the corner of the room. I turned to study it. Fear gripped my heart as I found myself gazing at a nine-foot tall ominous presence. It was not shaped like a person, but was without form — a huge, black swirling mass of what appeared to be smoke. In retrospect, it reminded me of how the earth must have looked at the beginning of creation: dark and without form, void.

I blinked my eyes to see if it would go away, but it was still there. The bone-chilling fear grew stronger and began to envelope my entire body. I could not move. I could barely breathe. Have you ever been this afraid? I tried to wake up my husband. I pounded on him. Normally he would have awakened but not this time. Instead he continued to snore in peace! Why wouldn't he wake up when I needed him?

Suddenly, I heard in my spirit, ''This is something *you* have to take care of yourself.''

''Okay,'' I answered. Then, still feeling great fear and shortness of breath, I whispered almost inaudibly, ''In the Name of Jesus.'' Because I was so scared, I could barely get the words out. "In the Name of Jesus," I repeated timidly, "I bind you, Satan. In the Name of Jesus, you cannot harm my family. I apply the blood of Jesus Christ over my family." I realized this presence was the death angel. It was there for only one reason: to kill and destroy us.

This was the first time in my life I ever *really* realized that Satan was trying to kill us. (Remember, this was shortly after we had started Church on the Rock-North in Dallas. I believe the devil, among other reasons, wanted to stop the building of our church.)

I repeated with more boldness, "I apply the blood of Jesus over my life and my husband's life."

It is extremely important that *YOU* know how to engage in spiritual warfare.

"I apply the blood of Jesus over my son's life," I continued. "I apply the blood of Jesus over Ruby's life." (She was watching our son, Lance, in the next room.) I knew that someone closely associated with us was about to be attacked.

By the time I finished speaking, faith had replaced fear in my heart. Knowing that God had heard my prayers, I closed my eyes then opened them again, fully expecting that thing to be gone. It was still there.

The enemy is always around, "seeking whom he may devour" (I Peter 5:8). Many times he camouflages himself so we cannot detect him. In a later chapter, however, I will show you how to recognize your camouflaged enemy.

Although the evil presence did not leave our hotel room that night, I had a peace that my prayers had defeated it; so I rolled over and went to sleep (very soundly, I might add).

*Introduction*

The next day I remembered what had happened, but never told Lawrence — until the Lord called my name out loud in our bedroom. Without fully understanding either experience, Lawrence and I pondered the meaning of these events, trusting the Lord to reveal the truth in His timing.

Why did I experience this demonic manifestation? Was it so I could tell a good story? No, it happened to me for very specific reasons.

# 1
# Know that a Woman's Place Is in Armor

You might think that a woman's place is to be frilly, soft, and sweet. This is not necessarily so. A woman's place is in armor. Christian women today must prepare for war on every front — spiritually.

What do I mean by the term *war*? *Webster's Unabridged Dictionary* defines the noun *war* as:

- Open armed conflict between...parties...carried on by force of arms...
- A conflict of arms between hostile parties or nations

As a verb, *war* means:

- ...To carry on hostilities...
- To contend
- To strive...[1]

Notice the key elements here by which war can be recognized: *conflict, hostility, strife.* This is true not only of physical war, but also of spiritual war.

If you have been hit with conflict or hostility from a person, remember what Ephesians 6:12 tells you:

---

[1]*Webster's New Universal Unabridged Dictionary,* ed. Jean L. McKechnie and others (New York: Simon and Schuster, 1983), p. 2059.

> **For we wrestle not against flesh and blood [people], but against principalities, against powers, against the rulers of the darkness of this world, against spiritual wickedness in high places.**

When you see conflict, hostility, or strife, know that spiritual warfare is taking place in your life. Always remember that the people who seem to cause you harm are not your enemies. Instead, the *spiritual forces* behind those people are your true enemies.

Every woman must recognize that she is in a daily spiritual battle for:

- Her physical life
- Her spiritual growth
- Her mind, emotions, and will
- Her family and other treasured relationships
- Her job, if she works outside the home
- And everything that is valuable to her

We all face spiritual warfare daily. A real enemy is trying to steal, kill, and destroy in your life (John 10:10, NASB). If you recognize this, then you are one giant step ahead of many Christians.

## Why Are Women Better Prey?

The reason I feel strongly impressed to direct this teaching toward women is that we are a mighty resource in the Body of Christ, which has been virtually untapped!

Many of us came from traditional church backgrounds where we learned that women are to stay in the background while the men minister; but, I declare to you today that God has called you into ministry, too. When God saved you, He called you into service for Him. For too long the enemy has led women to believe that they do not have ministries.

*Know that a Woman's Place Is in Armor*

In Galatians 3:28 (NKJV), God's Word says: ''...There is neither male nor female; for you are all one in Christ Jesus.'' Jesus spoke to *all* believers when He said, ''Go into all the world and preach the gospel to all creation'' (Mark 16:15, NASB). God has called every man, woman, and child in Christ to be a minister of the Gospel.

**Now all these things are from God, who reconciled us to Himself through Christ, and gave us the ministry of reconciliation,**

**namely, that God was in Christ reconciling the world to Himself, not counting their trespasses against them, and He has committed to us the word of reconciliation.**

**Therefore, we are ambassadors for Christ, as though God were entreating through us; we beg you on behalf of Christ, be reconciled to God.**

**II Corinthians 5:18-20 (NASB)**

I am not belittling the role of men. God's Word tells us that the man is the leader of his family. However, God has called you, as a woman, to be a co-laborer with your husband (if you are married) or with Christ (if you are single).

You are a gauge in your home. When the enemy attacks, you can choose to fight him spiritually with the weapons I will share in later chapters. Or you can turn to your emotions and fight back in the physical realm by losing your temper, yelling at your children, or not walking in love toward your husband. **You control the climate in your home by your reactions to your husband, children, and the enemy's attacks.**

To understand why he often chooses to tempt women, let's study a few of the first women in the Bible to face spiritual conflict. I want you to see what a powerful force you are as a woman — for good or for evil.

## Satan Wisely Attacked the First Woman

Why do you think Satan singled out Eve and tempted her? Why did mankind's enemy pursue the first *woman*? Why didn't he go after the man? Satan knew his gain would be greater if he could cause the woman to turn her back on God's Word.

> **And the Lord God commanded the man [Adam], saying, "From any tree of the garden you may eat freely;**
>
> **but from the tree of the knowledge of good and evil you shall not eat, for in the day that you eat from it you shall surely die."**
>
> **Then the Lord God said, "It is not good for the man to be alone; I will make him a helper suitable for him."**
>
> **Genesis 2:16-18 (NASB)**

Do you realize that God had not yet created Eve when He commanded Adam to avoid this tree? When the serpent later tempted Eve to eat the forbidden fruit, she replied that they could eat everything except the fruit of this tree. Evidently Adam had explained God's commandment to her. However, it appears that Eve had merely *heard from Adam* about God's Word concerning the tree. It is not recorded that she actually had a *first-hand revelation* about what God had said for her life. Eve replied to the serpent:

> **"But of the fruit of the tree which is in the midst of the garden, God has said, 'You shall not eat it, nor shall you touch it, lest you die.'"**
>
> **Genesis 3:3 (NKJV)**

*Know that a Woman's Place Is in Armor*

Eve perhaps hadn't heard God's Word for herself. Therefore, the enemy could deceive and trick her. Here is my point.

Many married women today rely too heavily on their husbands to make the right decisions for them. Often, however, when they face great conflicts in their families, their husbands are not home to help. Single Christian women, on the other hand, usually know that they are accountable to God for their decisions. Whether you are married or single, you are accountable to God for your actions and attitudes.

I truly believe that you cannot live on the revelation of anyone or anything else:

- Your husband
- Your parents
- Your heritage
- Your pastor
- Or your pastor's wonderful wife (Ha! Ha!)

You simply cannot live on anyone else's relationship with God or revelation about what He has said for your life. You must know and hear it for yourself. When the enemy comes to tempt you, that revelation will equip you so you can scream at the devil, ''No! I will not touch that! No, that area is wrong.''

Although Eve was the main target of temptation, I do not totally blame her for the fall. I believe that Adam should have been stronger. After Eve took a bite of the forbidden fruit, she handed it to Adam. He could have said, ''Woman, don't! Don't touch that! Don't eat that!'' However, it is not recorded in the Scripture that Adam struggled or resisted; he simply ate as Eve suggested.

What happened when Adam and Eve succumbed to the enemy's temptation and ate the forbidden fruit? It affected their entire household. Eve's family followed her direction.

> Then the eyes of both of them were opened, and they knew that they were naked; and they sewed fig leaves together and made themselves coverings.
>
> And they heard the sound of the Lord God walking in the garden in the cool of the day, and Adam and his wife hid themselves from the presence of the Lord God among the trees of the garden.
>
> Then the Lord God called to Adam and said to him, "Where are you?"
>
> So he said, "I heard Your voice in the garden, and I was afraid because I was naked; and I hid myself."
>
> And He said, "Who told you that you were naked? Have you eaten from the tree of which I commanded you that you should not eat?"
>
> Then the man said, "The woman whom You gave to be with me, she gave me of the tree, and I ate." [We all want to blame others for our mistakes and failures!]
>
> And the Lord God said to the woman, "What is this you have done?" The woman said, "The serpent deceived me, and I ate."
>
> **Genesis 3:7-13 (NKJV)**

When Adam and Eve followed the enemy's way of thinking — when they acted it out — they lost everything of value to them.

*Know that a Woman's Place Is in Armor*

- Adam and Eve — and all of mankind — lost their relationship with God. No longer did the first couple walk with Him in the cool of the day.
- They lost their prosperity and provision.
- They lost their peace. (Fear replaced peace.)
- They eventually lost their son's life.

## A Woman Is a Powerful Force in Her World

Throughout the Bible, there are many women whose actions greatly affected their families and loved ones. One example is in I Kings 21:25 (NKJV). Ahab did many wicked things in the sight of the Lord because of the actions of Jezebel, his wife.

**But there was no one like Ahab who sold himself to do wickedness in the sight of the Lord, because Jezebel his wife *stirred* him up.**

Think about the power of a wife to stir up her husband to do wrong. I have heard it said that the man is the head of the home, but the woman is the neck which turns the head. The wife has a great impact upon the actions of her household; unintentionally she can stir others up for evil behavior.

God's Word says in Proverbs 14:1 that a wise woman builds her house, but a foolish woman tears it apart with her own hands. Be wise. Don't tear your household apart by your own actions and attitudes.

Where are you headed? Is your family headed in the wrong direction? You can change that course. You have the power within you through Jesus Christ to turn your life and your family members' lives around to a better course.

Whatever Satan uses to bring destruction, God can use to bring great victory. Through woman, Satan brought the destruction of all of mankind; but through woman, God sent Jesus Christ to save the world. He can turn *your* situation around.

Knowledge is potential power. Do not be ignorant of the enemy's devices (II Corinthians 2:11). Hosea 4:6 says, ''My people are destroyed for lack of knowledge....'' That is not going to be true of you, if I can help it. You are going to be a mighty woman in armor!

# 2
# Master "Spiritual Warfare 101"

I started dabbling in the occult when I was about 11 years old, although my family and I didn't know that it was the occult. My girl friends and I often went to slumber parties, where we played with ouija boards, did levitations, and held seances all in the name of fun. (Perhaps you did this, too. If so, you must denounce all these activities. I will show you how through the Proclamation at the end of this book. See Appendix B.)

While these activities appeared to be innocent games, they were actually open doors for Satan to come into our lives. We were giving him legal permission to enter our lives.

You must understand the destruction the devil can bring to your children's lives in seemingly innocent ways. You can often prevent evil from infiltrating your family by paying close attention to the activities of your children.

My girl friends introduced me into witchcraft. It is known as the pagan religion, *wicca,* deceptively called the "white magic of God." This is totally false; wicca is in no way associated with the Lord God.

(In 1990 at a Larry Lea crusade in San Francisco, I met the leader of the pagans before he converted to Christ. He did not project God at all. He had a big pentagram on the front of his shirt with a black collar, white hair, and a black glove with metal studs on it. He was scary looking — not godly at all. As a result of that crusade, this man genuinely accepted Christ. We were in Santa Cruz not long ago, and he came to hear my husband preach. We met with him and found that God had miraculously transformed him. Praise God!)

As a young girl dabbling in the occult, I saw powerful manifestations of evil, some of which my mother also experienced. All of this caused me to know the reality of spiritual powers in high places — darkness (Ephesians 6:12). Although I did not yet know much about the Word of God, I sensed that this was not of Him. I knew that it was evil. This knowledge prompted me to give my life to Jesus Christ. I have engaged in spiritual warfare ever since.

After I became a Christian, strange things began to happen to me. For example, once on a college campus I was quietly sitting down, minding my own business. A man walked over, glared at me, and said in an eerie voice, ''You are a Christian.'' Then he began to curse at me. Nothing in the natural realm would have made him think I was a Christian; I did not have a cross, a Bible, or anything else that would have indicated this.

Other strange incidents happened. The girl who was trying to get me into witchcraft became heavily involved in the occult. Instead I became a Christian. After a few years of not seeing her, she showed up at our house one day, wanting to study with me for a class she was taking.

Surprised to see her, I agreed, ''Okay, fine.'' We put our books down. My mom was sitting at the kitchen table where we were going to study.

For no apparent reason, the girl asked, ''Coral, why is it that the church today doesn't have the power that the first church had?'' It shocked me to hear her ask such a question. She had been raised agnostic and had never gone to church.

"What do you mean?" I asked. "I believe the church does have the power that the first church had."

She replied quickly, "You mean, you believe that you have power to cast out devils and heal the sick?"

"Oh, yes. Absolutely!" I said boldly and confidently. "In Jesus' Name, I believe that."

Sensing the authority in my voice, the girl suddenly grew pale. Her eyes looked like golf balls. She grabbed her books and mumbled, "I've got to go!" She stood up, ran out of the house, and left the front door wide open.

My mother, who did not believe in casting out devils at the time, asked "What was that?"

"Mom," I replied, "you just saw a real demon possessed person. You just saw a real manifestation."

Then, suddenly I realized what had happened. Fear gripped my heart. Shaking, I ran to the front door, pulled it closed, hurriedly locked it, and breathed a sigh of relief.

"Well that's going to do a lot of good," my mother said, jokingly. "Trying to lock out the devil?"

I was a young woman of faith and power for only a few moments. Since that time, however, I have grown in the Word and in faith. I understand who I am in Christ and realize the power I have as a joint heir with Him. I do not have mere textbook knowledge about spiritual warfare. This is where God has placed me and is choosing to use me at this time.

## Tear Down the Strongholds over Your City

I received my first insight into spiritual warfare in approximately 1980 — before the teachings on this subject became popular or even known. My husband and I were pastoring our very first church. I did not know anything about spiritual warfare. At that time, the message commonly taught in the Body of Christ was faith and blessings.

The mass suicide of the followers of Jim Jones had recently happened in Guyana. As a result, the townspeople were skeptical of nondenominational churches. Ours was one of the city's first Charismatic churches.

Lawrence and I were experiencing a great deal of persecution in this small town in East Texas in the middle of the "Baptist Bible Belt." People were lying about us. It was shocking to find out that Christians outside our church were circulating most of these lies. I had never experienced anything like this in my life before.

To be honest, I became bitter about these people. I thought, "How in the world do they call themselves Christians when they're lying and being so mean? These people cannot be Christians." I found myself becoming very angry at them. However, deep in my heart, I knew they were well-meaning people, who did not know any better.

Have you ever had someone not treat you kindly? Have you become angry at them because of it? We all have. Well, I knew that I should not harbor these feelings. How could I be a good pastor's wife and honestly say, "God, bless you" when I saw these lying Christians? I couldn't. Something had to change, and the easiest thing to change was me. So I went to the Lord in prayer with my husband.

As we were praying, I saw one of the first visions that I have ever had. In my vision, a hard dome — like an eggshell — completely covered the city where we were pastoring. I did not understand what it meant. (See Figure A.)

**Figure A:** Vision of Spiritual Powers over Our City

Then, as we continued to pray and praise God, I saw this hard shell begin to crack. As we prayed with authority in the Name of Jesus, I saw big chunks fall out of this hard covering over our city. There had been very little light over the city until then; but as those chunks fell out, light began to stream in through the holes in the covering.

I asked, "Lord, what is this?" (If this were to happen to me today, I would understand what it meant, because of other experiences I've had. However, this was the first time I had ever seen or heard anything about spiritual warfare.)

The Lord showed me what this vision meant. The eggshell covering represented the spirit or principality over our area. This was the strong man over our region. It was a spirit of religion and a spirit of poverty. Suddenly, I knew that the people who were treating us badly were *not* our enemies. I realized that we were fighting the principality and power of the air over our region. He was fighting us — to discourage and stop us.

At that point, we started praying effectively against the powers of darkness over our city. We began to bind the enemy. What I am about to tell you is fact; I am not speaking "evangelistically." Within one year, our church attendance actually doubled. Within four years we were having more than 1,000 people coming to a Charismatic, spirit-filled church; this had never happened before in that entire region. We built a new facility on the interstate. We were asked to be on the Chamber of Commerce. It all began with two steps:

1. We first recognized WHO the enemy was. It was NOT the people in the city, but the spirits influencing those people.
2. Then we acted in faith on what I saw in my vision. We began to tear down the strongholds over our city.

*Master "Spiritual Warfare 101"*

# Recognize Demonic Activity in Your City

How does this pertain to you? I have shared this as a warning. Frank Peretti wrote two very true-to-life novels depicting the reality of this kind of demonic power, *This Present Darkness* and *Piercing the Darkness.*

I want you to understand that real spiritual influences exist where you live. The principalities and spirits are different in the various areas of each city, state, and nation of the world. Most people are not aware of these evil forces, which greatly affect how people look at life and how they respond to different situations. If you are not aware of these forces in your city, and if you do not guard your mind — whether you are a Christian or not — you can fall prey to these spirits.

Different types of sin are more prevalent in San Francisco, for example, than perhaps in Miami; and other sins more prevalent in Miami than elsewhere. The same is true for different regions of the country and different nations. Why? If people don't keep their minds girded up with the Word of Truth, the spirits of the air over their area can affect how they see life and what they desire.

For example, the principalities over North Dallas, where I live, include greed, materialism, pride, religion, immorality, drug addiction, murder, and others. These evil spirits affect not only the sinners, but also many Christians. You might think, "No! Not us." The statistics tell us otherwise.

The recent book *Vital Signs* reports that of Christian households hooked into cable television, 23% subscribe to pornographic channels. Here is the shocking statistic: this is the same percentage for the nation as a whole.[1] The enemy has tricked Christians into being just like the world.

---

[1] "The War within Continues," *Leadership,* IX (Winter 1988), 28.

"Sales of hard-core porn videos... more than doubled from 1983 to 1986."[2] Even ministers under stress are succumbing to temptation. Of the pastors responding to a recent survey, "20% said they look at sexually oriented media (in print, video, or movies) at least once a month."[3] The salt has lost its savor.

Let's declare, "From now on, Devil, NO MORE!" When worldly thoughts start plaguing our minds — when these things try to push us and mold us into the world's way of thinking — let's be aware of what is causing us to think this way. Let's stop the devil before he can create strongholds in our lives.

The devil wants to destroy us. The Word of God says that he has come to smite the shepherd and scatter the flock (Zechariah 13:7, Matthew 26:31, Mark 14:27). The ultimate objective of Satan is to scatter and nullify the power of a united church. In unity there is strength.

In the North Dallas area, we have seen prominent pastors fall into sexual immorality and other sins such as attempted murder. We have seen scandal after scandal rock the church leaders in a ten-mile radius of our church.

I believe that these men began as dedicated men of God, but did not believe or recognize the enemy of their souls. They did not know that an enemy was engaging them in spiritual warfare.

When I encountered the death angel in August of 1989, I realized what kind of an enemy we were up against in this city. However, I also understood more clearly than ever before who makes us victorious. It is only by the grace of God that any of us stands! If you are going to be victorious,

---

[2] *Ibid.*, p. 24.
[3] *Ibid.*

*Master "Spiritual Warfare 101"*

you too must realize that you have a crafty and merciless foe, who is powerless against the mighty Lord Jesus Christ in *YOU*.

In the early to mid 1980s, a friend of mine told me something very shocking. However, when I think about all the events that have happened since that time, it is easy to believe her story.

My friend was going on a trip and stumbled across a group of satanists. They were "fasting and praying" for the destruction of prominent Christian leaders and their families.

You might recall that in the early 1980s and throughout that decade, the church wanted to hear about blessing, riches, and prosperity. Meanwhile the powers of darkness were seriously waging war against us and taking our territory. Why did they desire the destruction of the families of prominent ministers? It was because Satan is out to smite the shepherds and scatter the flock.

What is his objective after he attacks the shepherds? You, the sheep! That's right. So I ask, for your sake, that you pray for your pastor and his family. Woman of God, we need to get serious about this. We really do.

We have a real enemy. It is extremely important that we as the Body of Christ join together to declare the Word of God over our families, cities, states, nations, and the world. We must speak the truth of the Word, not the lies of the devil. (See the examples listed in Appendix C.)

The purpose of this book is to first make the Body of Christ aware of the battle we are in and then to solicit your help in waging war on the devil and all his forces.

The powers of darkness are trying to destroy not only Christians, but all of mankind. These are the last of the last days. Now he is pulling out all the stops. The onslaught is on, but remember you have the Greater One inside of you! Amen.

## The Enemy Has Taken America Captive

Self-inflected personal destruction, sickness, and crime is alarmingly high today. Bulimia, anorexia, drug addiction, and alcoholism are all on the rise. Treatment centers are experiencing an all-time high demand; most have waiting lists.

- A report in 1987 showed that over one-half million (598,079) people in the United States were cared for in alcoholism and drug abuse treatment facilities.[4]

- The latest figures available indicate that expenditures for mental health facilities were nearly $18.5 billion ($18,459,000,000) in 1987 alone. I thank God for those centers, but there should not be this many people needing treatment in centers.[5]

- The total amount spent on health services and supplies in the United States more than doubled in the eight years between 1980 and 1988: from $249.1 billion to $539.9 billion.[6]

- "According to the American Heart Association, the estimated cost of cardiovascular diseases in 1991 will be $101.2 billion...."[7]

---

[4]U.S. Bureau of the Census, *Statistical Abstract of the United States: 1990* (110th edition) Washington, D.C., 1990, p. 122.

[5]*The World Almanac and Book of Facts 1991,* ed. Mark S. Hoffman and others (New York: Pharos Books, 1990), p. 846.

[6]*Ibid.,* p. 844.

[7]*Ibid.,* p. 845.

*Master "Spiritual Warfare 101"*

The crimes perpetrated by the devil against Americans continue to rise.

- The growth in the number of AIDS cases from 1988 to 1989 is startling, especially among heterosexuals (36% increase) and newborns (38%).[8]
- The most recent statistics indicate that the number of legal abortions in the United States during 1985 alone was nearly 1.6 million.[9] It is a shame that abortion is so rampant in our nation. Besides being murder, there are many families on waiting lists all over America, wanting to adopt these children.
- "Overall, the number of crimes committed nationwide rose to 14.25 million in 1989."[10]

What does all of this mean? A real enemy has been at work destroying people's minds, emotions, and families. We are a hurting country. We have a sick society. These are merely signs that all is not well in America. Yet, we are supposedly "one nation under God." Do we exhibit the signs of being a nation under God? No, but we are going to turn that around in Jesus' Name!

## It's Time for War

God has not called my husband and me to sit back on our laurels. Yes, we are having a great move of God here at Church on the Rock-North in Dallas. I am excited about what God is doing here, but it is for a purpose.

---

[8]*Ibid.*, p. 846
[9]U.S. Bureau of the Census, p. 72.
[10]*The World Almanac and Book of Facts 1991*, p. 848.

I believe it is for the same purpose that He has directed you to read this book: so you and I can make a difference in our society. We are to be the salt of the earth. We are to be the light of the world. I pray that this book will somehow help the Body of Christ to shine the way God has called us to shine and join together to wage war upon the devil and his demons.

This is war! If you are going to win, you must treat it as such. No military unit commander would ever go to war without first:

- Recognizing where the battlefield is
- Knowing the enemy, his allies, and their forces
- Understanding the enemy's capabilities
- Studying the enemy's battle tactics
- Identifying the enemy's weapons
- Planning to exploit the enemy's weaknesses
- Knowing who his own allies are
- Understanding the capabilities of his own forces
- Preparing a battle plan and communicating it to his own forces
- Realizing the power of his weapons
- Utilizing the strengths of his forces

Remember, the Bible says in Hosea 4:6, ''My people are destroyed for lack of knowledge....'' It is time for the people of God to stop being destroyed. I have written this book to help you receive important knowledge that will prevent your destruction. Throughout the next several chapters, we will discuss all of the above strategies of war.

# Part II
# What Are Your Enemy's Capabilities?

# 3
# Give No Place to the Enemy of Your Soul

The Lord once gave one of His servants a powerful vision to reach the world. Secular and Christian audiences alike acknowledged this man for his work. The television program "This is Your Life" featured him in the 1950s. He did great works for God, such as funding orphanages in Korea and other powerful works all around the world.

This man's wife was a good woman, but she had a fear — a fear that grew and grew. She was afraid of flying. Since her husband's ministry called for him to fly continually all over the world, she never traveled with him. Instead, she allowed the fear to control her life; she did not take command over it with the help of the Lord. Consequently, she allowed her fear to separate her from her husband; they spent many years apart.

Your marriage is like your relationship with the Lord. If you never spend any time with Him, you will not feel close to Him. Right?

This woman allowed her fear of flying to grip her heart so much that she and her husband finally separated. They had several children; and one of their daughters eventually committed suicide.

What would have happened to this woman and her family if she had defeated this fear? She could have said, "Wait a minute. God is on my husband's side. He called my husband to do this. I know this airplane is not going to go down, because my husband has not finished God's work yet." If she had known the reality that God is true and faithful, and that He protects His children, imagine what could have happened in that family.

My point is simply this: there is a real enemy trying to steal, kill, and destroy in your life. It's time that you stand up and declare to your enemy, "The strength and power of Jesus Christ enables me to do all things. No more will I allow you, Satan, to destroy in my life through fear or any other demonic attack."

Perhaps you don't have a fear of flying; but maybe the enemy is trying to steal, kill, and destroy in another area of your life. It's time today to say, "NO MORE! I resist you, Satan, in the Name of Jesus." When you do that, he has to flee (James 4:7). Through Jesus Christ you can take charge of your life today.

In Ecclesiastes 3:1 (NASB) God's Word says, "There is an appointed time for everything. And there is a time for every event under heaven...."

Now is the season for war: first the natural then the spiritual (I Corinthians 15:46). In the natural, we recently achieved a great victory in the Middle East crisis. Likewise, I believe in the spirit realm, a great victory is coming to you and to me. Read the end of The Book: we win!

The Body of Christ has been in basic training. Now I believe it is time for us to arise as the "Special Forces" in God's army to take back everything that the enemy has stolen.

Psalm 144:1 (NASB) says, "Blessed be the Lord, my rock, Who trains my hands for war, And my fingers for battle." If you do not believe that He trains you for spiritual warfare, you are wrong. He is training you now even as you read this book.

What area in your life have you been struggling with?

- Maybe it is your marriage.
- Maybe you have a low self-esteem, and it almost seems to overtake you at times.
- Maybe you are battling depression; you get so low that you feel like nothing could be as low as you are. I don't believe that it's God's will for any believer in Jesus Christ to be depressed all the time.
- Maybe worry is plaguing you.
- Maybe anger is plaguing you; that is not God's best for you.
- Maybe you are fretting over your financial condition. You are constantly lacking enough money to pay your bills.

These are all signals of one fact: you are at war with an enemy that is trying to steal, kill, and destroy God's best in your life.

## Who Is Your Enemy?

Both in physical and spiritual war, you must know who your enemy is. In the Vietnam War, many U.S. soldiers died because they did not recognize the enemy and they let their guards down. Enemy civilian mothers, children, and elderly deceived our unsuspecting troops with booby traps. In this guerilla warfare, our soldiers did not recognize the danger because the enemy did not attack in military uniforms with machine guns.

In spiritual war, many people let their guards down because they don't see the devil in a red suit with a pitchfork. For too long, Satan has disguised himself. We often see cartoons, portraying him as a comedian figure: with a long tail, a pitchfork, and sharp, pointy horns. Children laugh at these kinds of illustrations of the devil.

For years the devil has deceived the Body of Christ. Many Christians do not believe there is a real devil, a real enemy. They unknowingly allow him to come into their lives to steal, kill, and destroy.

The Bible tells us, "Above all else, guard your heart, for it is the wellspring of life" (Proverbs 4:23, NIV). We must be on guard at all times to give no place to the devil in our lives. Throughout this book, I will show you how to do this.

You must remember the real enemy is *not* people, but the spirits influencing them. If you don't learn anything else from this book, learn this one point! People are not your problem. Ephesians 6:12 in *The Living Bible* vividly explains this point well:

**For we are not fighting against people made of flesh and blood, but against persons without bodies — the evil rulers of the unseen world, those mighty satanic beings and great evil princes of darkness who rule this world; and against huge numbers of wicked spirits in the spirit world.**

Understand that you are *not* fighting human beings. Mentally, you might know this; but when put to the test, how do you respond? This will show what is really in your heart. Study how you react when someone does you wrong. What do you do when you feel attacked in the following ways:

- You do not get the promotion that you know you deserved.

*Give No Place to the Enemy of Your Soul*

- Your boss abuses you.
- Your teenager says a cutting remark to you.
- Your husband does not treat you lovingly or makes jokes about the way you look.

It is time that you realize you are not fighting flesh and blood. If you and your teenager are not communicating well, you might feel that you don't even know your own child. How then, can you possibly reach that teenager and speak wisdom into his or her life?

If you suddenly realize that your own ''flesh and blood'' will not listen to you, it hurts. If your teenager says horrible things to you, yes, it hurts; but remember that you are not fighting your teenager. You are fighting spiritual forces that are trying to influence his or her life.

It is time that you take spiritual weapons to tear down those spiritual forces, rather than sighing and merely saying, ''Oh, well, my teenager is just going through a phase.''

I have heard about parents who did not fully recognize the magnitude of the problems in their teenagers' lives. The parents knew that they were acting a little strange, had bizarre drawings in their books, and were listening to record albums with skulls on the front. However, the parents failed to recognize that these were demonic symbols and never intervened; they thought it was ''just a phase.'' Many of these teenagers became so entangled in satanic activities that they eventually committed murder or suicide.

It is time that you recognize the signs around you and make a stand, declaring, ''No more!'' Realize that you can take authority over the principalities, and powers, and rulers in high places.

## Satan Is a Master of Deception

Your enemy is Satan himself and his demons. Jesus explained that Satan is a master of deception.

**Ye are of your father the devil, and the lusts of your father ye will do. He was a murderer from the beginning, and abode not in the truth, because there is no truth in him. When he speaketh a lie, he speaketh of his own: for he is a liar, and the father of it.**

**John 8:44**

This reminds me of the phrase "a wolf in sheep's clothing." That wolf looks, acts, and sounds like a sheep; he tries very hard to deceive all of the real sheep. However, if the sheep knew his true identity, they would run for their lives.

Our spiritual enemy acts the same way. He disguises himself as good — as an *angel of light* (II Corinthians 11:14). He tries to deceive us into allowing him entrance into our lives to steal, kill, and destroy. His true identity, however, is the *father of lies* (John 8:44).

Has someone been lying in your ear, trying to get you to doubt God and His Word? Perhaps a doctor has diagnosed your case and said, "There's no hope for you." Maybe a parent or teacher told you, "You're too rotten. You will never amount to anything." Maybe even a "fellow Christian" has mocked you, saying, "You can't go to God with your problems. Look how you've failed. Look at your sin."

I want you to know who the author of these lies is. It is not God. *It is not God!* Stop listening to the words the enemy is throwing at you. Recognize where they come from and resist them; and remember, the people used in speaking such things to you are *not* your enemies.

Remember, Proverbs 14:1 (NASB) says:

**The wise woman builds her house, But the foolish tears it down with her own hands.**

Have you ever seen this happen? I have seen families that appear to have everything they could ever want, and yet they seem to be on a course of self-destruction. Why? Are people trying to destroy themselves? No, but someone is — Satan himself!

It is time that we recognize the forces that are trying to destroy families. A real enemy is trying to steal, kill, and destroy in your life; my life; and in the lives of every man, woman, and child on the face of the earth. We must not allow this to happen.

Unfortunately, many Christians do not even know that they are in spiritual warfare. In fact, many members of the Body of Christ do not even believe there is a spiritual world.

One of the greatest tactics an enemy can use against you is to deceive you into believing that he does not exist. In fact, Pierre Baudelaire said, "The Devil's most beautiful ruse is to convince us that he does not exist."[1] For example, if a thief wanted to rob someone's possessions, it would be extremely easy if he were invisible.

This is actually happening in the Body of Christ today, spiritually. It is as though Christians are saying, "I don't believe there is a thief in this house." As they watch their family relationships being stolen before their very eyes (like a television set being carried out the door), they are saying, "Nope! I don't see anyone. There's no enemy." As the thief

---

[1]Eugene H. Peterson, "Stumbling Across the Supernatural," *Leadership,* XII (Summer 1991), 90.

is carrying away everything of value to them, many Christians continue to be adamant that there is no enemy.

In the recent Persian Gulf War, many soldiers and civilians were afraid that chemical warfare would erupt. Do you know why? Chemical warfare is especially dangerous not only because it is deadly, but because it difficult to detect. Victims don't know that invisible chemicals are present, until it's too late. They cannot *see* an enemy. People think all is well until suddenly fatal symptoms appear and death is imminent.

This principle is true in spiritual warfare. The devil attacks unsuspecting victims. They think everything is fine until suddenly death comes — spiritual death. Their lives begin to dry up spiritually. There is hope for you, however, if you are in this condition now. In this book, I will show you how to get watered — how to be spiritually satisfied. The first step is to realize there is a devil. **I have written this book to declare to you today that you *do* have an enemy; he *does* exist; he is real; his name is Satan.**

However, the Bible declares, ''. . . Greater is he that is in you, than he that is in the world'' (I John 4:4). You don't have to be afraid of Satan and the powers of darkness if you are a born-again believer. I want you to know that you are much more powerful than he is, because greater is the Spirit of the Living God who dwells inside you.

If, on the other hand, you do not have Jesus Christ in your life today, Satan will batter you. He is a merciless enemy; he will destroy you if you do not have the power of God to defeat him in your life.

Turmoil, strife, and confusion filled my life before I accepted Jesus. I was powerless and had no control over

*Give No Place to the Enemy of Your Soul*

circumstances. As a believer now, however, I have power to overcome the enemy in Jesus' Name; every believer does. This *can* include *you*!

Perhaps you're not sure that you're really a Christian — bound for heaven. Go to Appendix A (at the end of this book) for assurance and a NEW BEGINNING IN CHRIST JESUS! I will show you how to accept Jesus, so you can *always* be victorious in Him.

# 4
# Recognize the Battlefield

In the physical realm, guerilla warfare is deadly. Because of its camouflage and deception, this method of fighting causes confusion. When using guerilla warfare, an enemy can choose the *time* and the *location* of battle, thus gaining a physical advantage.

The 20th-century American military strategy states, "The best defense is a good offense." Being on the offensive allows the forces to choose the location and the time of battle to gain the advantage.

Likewise, in spiritual warfare, Satan tries to use deception and confusion to choose the location and time of his battle with you. However, did you know that God's Word gives *you* the advantage?

In His Word, God has already told you the *location* of your spiritual battlefield. It is in your mind. You now know the location. Now choose the *time* to fight. Don't wait for the enemy to attack you. Instead, take the offensive and attack him first. Keep him on the run!

## Understand the Times

Today the Body of Christ must be like the sons of Issachar in I Chronicles 12:32.

> **And of the children of Issachar, which were men that had understanding of the times, to know what Israel ought to do....**

These men understood the times. Do *you* know what time it is right now? Do you know what moments we are living in? We are living in the last days of time. We are seeing a tremendous increase in spiritual activity like never before.

The New Age movement and other false religions are on the rise. Advertised on national television at night are 900-toll numbers; you can now pay to call and become involved in the occult! These television commercials offer the services of tarot card readers and psychic advisors. You also can call to receive your daily personal horoscope reading. We as Christians should write to our congressional representatives and to television station managers to tell them we are outraged at this occult programming.

If someone had told me years ago that this would be on national television, I would have said, ''No way! This is America. We won't have witchcraft and voodoo on our television.'' However, it is now on our television sets every day. It's time that we realize, like the sons of Issachar, what time it is. It's time that we wake up and declare, ''No more! No more!'' We must begin to take back the ground that the enemy has stolen from us.

## Take the Offensive

Most Christians who engage in spiritual warfare are continually on the defensive. They fight back after the devil attacks. However, they don't understand there is more to spiritual warfare.

It's time for Christians to be on the offensive. It's time for you to fight offensively, to pull down the enemy's strongholds *before he attacks* again in your life, family, church, city, and nation. It's time for you to take the offensive; use

*Recognize the Battlefield*

the Sword of the Spirit to put the devil on the run. (We will discuss how to do this in detail in a later chapter.)

I have heard people say, ''It's too hard being a Christian on the front lines. I had it a lot easier when I was in the world. I didn't get attacked like this then. It's too hard here. I think I'll backslide and go into the world just a little bit, because this is too hard.''

What would have happened to our troops in the Persian Gulf War if they had given up? They could have said, ''Wait a minute, this war is too hard. I don't like this fighting business, and this sand is really getting old. I'm tired of eating these rations too. I think I'm just going to wander over to the enemy's side, because it's going to be a little bit easier over there.'' What would have happened to our troops? They would have been killed or taken hostage, chained, abused, and beaten. This is where many Christians are today, spiritually.

It's time for you to realize that you can't run away from God. Where can you go to get away from Him? Can you get away from God in the mountains, at sea, at work? No! He's there. He's everywhere. He will never leave nor forsake you (Hebrews 13:5).

You cannot get away from the devil either. It's time to realize that you cannot run away from problems. You must stand up, face them head on, and attack your enemy. Remember, greater is He that is in you, than he that is in the world — and this includes the devil (I John 4:4).

Several months ago, my husband, Lawrence, had a vision of Bob Mason, our associate pastor and worship leader. Lawrence saw Bob with his hands raised, worshipping God and facing his wife Debbie. (At this time, Bob and Debbie were fighting a serious battle against cancer for Debbie's life.)

Suddenly, as Bob worshipped the Lord, a horrible demon appeared behind Bob; I believe it was the death angel. However, Bob was oblivious to everything around him — including the demon. My husband could see that as Bob continued in deep worship of Almighty God, the death angel could not destroy Debbie.

Immediately when the demon saw my husband, it launched out to attack him. A strong fear enveloped my husband, and he said to himself, ''I have to run. I have to turn around and run.'' My husband looked over at Bob and saw that he was still deeply engrossed in worship; Bob did not know the demon was there. At that point, Lawrence said he knew in his spirit that if he ran, the demon would overtake him and kill him.

Suddenly, my husband knew what he should do: *attack* the demon. As he boldly stepped forward, do you know what happened? The demon, that had been attacking and trying to kill him, ran!

Through this vision, the Lord showed my husband two important revelations:

- Praise and worship unleash tremendous power.
- Christians must be aggressive in the spiritual realm.

Most Christians do not recognize the power they can unleash through praise and worship. What do the terms *praise* and *worship* mean? *Praise* is acknowledging the wonderful acts of God and declaring out loud who He is. *Worship* equips us to defeat the enemy.

The Greek word for worship is *proskuneo* (pros-koo-neh'-o). It comes from a word literally meaning ''to kiss.''[1] The ''kiss of worship'' is becoming totally engulfed with

---

[1] W. E. Vine, M.A., *Vine's Expository Dictionary of New Testament Words* (Peabody: Hendrickson Publishers, Unabridged Edition), p. 1258.

the Lord. When we stand before His throne in worship, everything we face in this life diminishes in His presence.

Power comes as we sing praises to God. This is a part of warfare that can be seen many times in the Old and New Testaments. It is also vital for spiritual warfare today.

While Bob continued in deep worship of Almighty God, the death angel could not destroy Debbie. In fact, as Bob continued to worship the Lord, he was totally oblivious to the very existence of the demon that was trying to kill his wife. Bob's praises seemed to block the demon from touching Debbie.

When *you* are in a prison made by the enemy, sing and praise God like the disciples did when they were in jail (Acts 16:22-26). The Lord sent an angel to deliver them! Let us open our hearts and mouths wide in worship and praise.

- SHOUT! For the Lord has given us the city!
- SHOUT! For the Lord has given you your family!
- SHOUT! For the Lord has given you the answer!
- SHOUT! For the Lord has given you the victory!

It's time that we stand up and fight him, declaring, ''No more! No more! Devil, you cannot have my life, my family, my church, my city, or my nation!''

You must take an offensive stand against the enemy. Don't run; he will overtake you. Don't take the defensive position; he will attack with full force when you least expect it. Begin attacking him. Take back what he has stolen. Declare the Lord's blessings in every area of your life. Attack *before* he attacks you in any of these areas:

- Finances
- Family
- Job

- Health
- Local church
- City
- Nation

Let him who steals steal no more (Ephesians 4:28)!

## Guard Your Mind

The devil attacks your mind. You must realize this. Romans 8:5-8 (NASB) says:

> **For those who are according to the flesh set their minds on the things of the flesh, but those who are according to the Spirit, the things of the Spirit.**
>
> **For the mind set on the flesh is death, but the mind set on the Spirit is life and peace,**
>
> **because the mind set on the flesh is hostile toward God; for it does not subject itself to the law of God, for it is not even able to do so;**
>
> **and those who are in the flesh cannot please God.**

Do you think more about money, things that you want to buy, places you want to go, and homes you want to live in? Or do you think more about the things of God, how good Jesus is; how good it is that He cleansed, washed, and forgave you; and how you can share Jesus with others so they can have peace that passes any circumstance? Where is your mind? What are you dwelling on most of the time?

If you dwell on the things of God, and you seek His kingdom first then *ALL* those things shall be added unto you (Matthew 6:33); but the enemy tries to tempt you into thinking about all the things that you want added to your life. If you do this, you won't get those things. The Lord

*Recognize the Battlefield*

knows that they will destroy you; those things have become idols in your life.

In the days that we are living in, nothing is more important than seeking the Lord Jesus Christ. Don't worry about things; He wants to bless you like a parent wants to bless his or her child. When I think of my son, Lance, I want to bless him with more things than he even desires — and that's a lot!

Your heavenly Father feels the same way about you; so quit dwelling on the things you want, what the economy is like, how you are going to pay your bills, what your body feels like, and what others think of you.

Start dwelling on the Lord, and then He will keep your mind and your heart in perfect peace. This is what the world is after. That's why there has been such a boom in the psychiatric hospitals. I am grateful for organizations like these that help people; I believe there is a real need for them.

However, I believe that many people who are spending $10,000 or $20,000 each month could save their money if they just said, "Wait a minute. I'm going to set my attention and affection on the Lord Jesus Christ." If people would do this, I believe they would be set free. I really do.

**Don't let the world around you squeeze you into its own mould, but let God re-make you so that your whole attitude of mind is changed....**
**Romans 12:2 (Phillips)**

Only with God's help can you accomplish this! You must first realize that your enemy, Satan, is trying to launch a mighty attack against your mind every day. However, you can cut him off at the pass by recognizing his weapons of attack. Let's discuss these in detail in the next chapters.

# 5
# Identify Your Enemy's Weapons

To fight effectively, you must know how to identify the enemy's weapons, whether in physical or spiritual warfare. Before we study this, I want you to keep in mind what the Word of God says about your enemy's weapons:

> "No weapon that is formed against you shall prosper; And every tongue that accuses you in judgment you will condemn.
>
> This is the heritage of the servants of the Lord,
>
> And their vindication is from Me," declares the Lord.
>
> Isaiah 54:17 (NASB)

As we study, remember that you have power over all the enemy's weapons in Jesus' Name. Some are obvious attacks:

- Sickness
- Sin
- Accidents
- Destruction
- Marital Problems
- Poverty

However, the enemy also camouflages his attacks on our minds. These are often difficult to detect and are the most dangerous. Many times we as believers are ignorant of his devices. The enemy can sneak up on us; and before we know it, he is devouring us. It is vital that we recognize his weapons.

In this and the next chapter, we will discuss the following demonic weapons:
- Idolatry, Spirit of Confusion
- Spirit of Religion
- Criticism of Others
- Conflict, Hostility, Strife
- Lukewarmness in Your Spiritual Walk
- Constant Temptation to Sin
- Negative Thoughts
- Accusations about Your Past Failures

## Idolatry, Spirit of Confusion

Why are cities and nations being overrun with violence, lust, child pornography, and addictions? Why are people burned out and over stressed? Why do we continually hear about stress management, dysfunctional families, and co-dependency?

Why do so many people have no vision for their lives except to eat, drink and be merry? Why is there no vision or long-term goals? Why do people want instant gratification, without caring about the long-term consequences?

Why has confusion and despair replaced hope and desire? There is an answer: *idolatry.* Idolatry? Yes, idolatry exists in 20th-century America!

Wherever there is a spirit or principality of idolatry there is confusion. It produces confusion in people, families, and governments. This is what we are seeing in America today. Isaiah 45:16 (NKJV) says:

*Identify Your Enemy's Weapons*

**They shall be ashamed and also disgraced, all of them; they shall go in confusion together, who are makers of idols.**

*Webster's Unabridged Dictionary* defines *idolatry* as "the worship of idols, images, etc.; excessive attachment...for some person or thing; admiration which borders on adoration."[1]

When you worship anything or anyone other than God, you become confused, lose direction and purpose for your life. The definition of *confuse* is "to mix up...to jumble...to perplex...to mistake the identity of."[2] When you worship idols, you mistakenly believe that an object or person can fill the need in your life that only God can satisfy.

What are the idols of 20th-century Americans? In our country, we have excessive attachments for money, sex, sports, music, drugs, and for things that make us feel good. All these things can become idols if we begin lusting after and are excessively attached to them.

Remember, we are not to be ignorant of the enemy's devices. One of Satan's weapons is to tempt you to worship something more than you worship God.

You might be thinking, *I don't worship anything more than God. I'm not excessively attached to money, sex, sports, music, drugs, or anything else. I don't have any of those in my life.*

---

[1] *Webster's New Universal Unabridged Dictionary,* ed. Jean L. McKechnie and others (New York: Simon and Schuster, 1983), p. 903.

[2] *Ibid.,* p. 383.

Be sure to check your heart. Is there anything that is more important to you than your relationship with God, or that is taking so much of your time that you do not have time for Him?

Do you have confusion in your life? Maybe you don't have clear direction or a vision for your life. Maybe you feel like you are in a whirlwind; confusion is swirling all around you, and you don't know which way to turn.

If so, perhaps there is a stronghold or an area — an idol — in your life that you are placing higher than your relationship with God. It could even be your business or your family. You must lay down anything that is trying to exalt itself over your relationship with God. Search your heart.

Today, right where you sit, you can turn to the Lord, the Author and Finisher of your faith (Hebrews 12:2). You can say to Him:

**No more! Lord, I place You first in my life. I ask Your forgiveness for getting my priorities out of order and for putting things above my relationship with You. I give this idol to You, and I ask You to help me to get my life in order.**

## Spirit of Religion

Another weapon that Satan often uses is the *spirit of religion*. God showed me in my vision that this was the problem in the town where we had our first church.

What is a spirit of religion? It is a demon of idolatry that causes confusion; a spiritual influence that causes people to place more credence in and to submit themselves to their own traditions and practices rather than allowing God to move powerfully in their midst.

Congregations under the influence of the spirit of religion will cling to their traditions — even if these practices are not biblically based — instead of allowing Jesus Christ to be the Lord and Ruler of their lives. People bound by this spirit will often make comments such as, ''That goes against my background,'' or ''We've *always* done it like this.''

This spirit also can influence Christians to criticize those who do not measure up to their human standards. II Timothy 3:4-5 says that men will become ''...lovers of pleasures more than lovers of God; Having a 'form' of godliness, but denying the power thereof....'' This is happening today in the Christian world.

The church must break the grips of this evil influence. We must be open-minded enough to say, ''Okay, Lord, I will do whatever You have called me do, and I won't criticize what You have called others to do. You are Lord of my life.'' When we let Him be Lord, we can accomplish anything with His power.

## Criticism of Others

A powerful weapon of the enemy to guard against is the *temptation to criticize others.* For too long, many Christians have eagerly listened to every sordid detail of gossip about other members in the Body of Christ, believing it was their Christian duty to correct the behavior of others.

Who is the author of criticism? Who tries to steal, kill, and destroy? Who tears down people instead of building them up? Satan himself.

Do you remember who wanted to free Barabbas and crucify Jesus? It was the pious, religious leaders of that day. A religious spirit had taken control of their lives.

Be careful when you feel you are justified in criticizing and judging others. If you can ridicule brothers and sisters in the Body of Christ, and not be gripped in your heart with sorrow (even if they are wrong), maybe a religious spirit is trying to dominate you and hinder your walk with Christ.

Here are several verses to remember if you have a tendency to do this. Jesus said:

> **"Judge not, that you be not judged.**
>
> **"For with what judgment you judge, you will be judged; and with the same measure you use, it will be measured back to you.**
>
> **"And why do you look at the speck in your brother's eye, but do not consider the plank in your own eye?**
>
> **"Or how can you say to your brother, 'Let me remove the speck out of your eye'; and look, a plank is in your own eye?**
>
> **"Hypocrite! First remove the plank from your own eye, and then you will see clearly to remove the speck out of your brother's eye...."**
> **Matthew 7:1-5 (NKJV)**

Don't focus on the faults of others. Instead, work on fixing your own. We all have a few to take care of. I certainly do not want to be judged harshly, so I try not to be critical of others. You need to say, "No! No! I refuse to criticize others, even if they are wrong." **Don't *say* it; *pray* it.**

Watch for any negative thoughts about others. God never sees people in a negative light. The ones who do *not* know Him, He sees lost and hurting. Those who *do* know Him, He sees covered by the blood of Jesus Christ.

Yes, there are many people in the Body of Christ who have intentionally hurt others. Maybe a "fellow Christian"

*Identify Your Enemy's Weapons*

has hurt you. I am not saying that you should wear blinders, but you *must* forgive.

If God forgives them, who are you and I not to forgive them? Right? Who are you to take a splinter out of someone else's eye when you have a big beam in your eye? In other words, your vision is hindered when you have a big beam in your eye.

I had to walk through this a few years ago. I had to forgive some people who had truly hurt me. They were wrong, and I argued, "But God, they are wrong. They have hurt me." I wanted to stay in self-pity.

However, the Lord corrected me, "Wait a minute, Coral. You *have* to forgive them. If you don't forgive them, I can't forgive you" (Matthew 6:14-15). I knew I had several things in my life for which I needed forgiveness, so I forgave these people. What a wonderful freedom I felt.

How about you? Can you afford to allow the spirit of judgment or criticism against others, who are disobedient to the Lord, to rule in your life?

When thoughts of bitterness, wrath, anger, or self-pity hit you, watch out! You must remove these from your life so your prayers will not be hindered.

Are *you* (or have you ever been) involved in any activity or group that is critical to any members of the Body of Christ or to a local church? The Holy Spirit does not order this; the very author of confusion and strife does — Satan.

If you have ever done this, what should you do? Repent. Begin to become a restorer instead of a destroyer in your church, home, marriage, family, job. Bring healing wherever you go.

Allow your actions to uplift others. Walk in forgiveness. Be a Christian, not only in word but in deed. Have an open, gracious spirit. Don't allow the enemy to get you hooked into any kind of spirit of religion.

The Body of Christ must begin to fight *for* one another rather than *against* each other. In unity, we as Christians have the power to tear down strongholds in our lives and refuse to give Satan place to manipulate us. We do not have to speak evil about other people any longer. We now have the freedom and liberty to love — no matter what.

## Conflict, Hostility, and Strife

As we discussed in the first chapter, you can recognize spiritual warfare by *conflict, hostility, and strife* in your life. One of the most powerful verses in the Bible is James 3:16, which says, "For where envying and strife is, there is confusion and every evil work." You must guard this area of your life. Strife leads to confusion. Why do we find ourselves in such confusion? We are at war.

In the very first battle of this spiritual war, Satan tried to confuse Eve by contradicting God's Word. He tempted her to take control of her life, thus taking charge of her destiny instead of trusting God's plan for her life.

What happened in Eve's family as a result? Conflict, hostility, and strife entered. She and Adam became confused. She succumbed to the enemy's devices and eventually her son Cain killed his brother, Abel.

This is happening in countless families across this nation, but we as Christians can *do* something about it. We can stand up to the devil and fight for our families.

As the woman in your home, *you* have an extremely powerful weapon to stop conflict, hostility, and strife from gaining a stronghold in your family.

Whenever you see evidence of this kind of attack, stop it with love. Take every opportunity to pour love into the

*Identify Your Enemy's Weapons*

members of your family, for love covers a multitude of sins (I Peter 4:8). Love reciprocates love. When you give it, it comes back. Later, we will further discuss this powerful weapon that you possess.

You also need to pull down the strongholds of conflict, hostility, and strife where you work. Before working full-time in the ministry, I worked in the office of a secular business. Miracles happened when I began to pray and bind Satan in that place. My boss accepted Jesus as his Savior after I worked there for three years. I was straight forward with what I believed, but not offensive. (I didn't wave Bibles or tracts in their faces.)

God will give you wisdom where you work. The key is to remember that the people you are having conflicts with are not your enemies. You are not wrestling against flesh and blood. Realize who you are dealing with.

There are several other weapons Satan likes to use against Christians. We will briefly discuss these in the following chapter.

# 6
# Break the Chains of Strongholds

What you spend your time thinking about and dwelling on is extremely important. I once heard someone say:

- Sow a thought, reap a word.
- Sow a word, reap an act.
- Sow an act, reap a habit.
- Sow a habit, reap a character.
- Sow a character, reap a destiny!

Where is your destiny headed? Where is your family headed? If you know it is not headed where God would have it headed, stop! Change your mind. Repent. Turn to God. Go in the opposite direction from where you are headed, and see what God will do with your life.

Your destiny, fulfillment, and life expectations begin with your thought life. God wants you to dream big for your life. **He wants you to believe Him for the impossible because He specializes in the impossible.**

You have a glorious destiny in God. In Him, your life will be better than you could ever make it on your own. His Word guarantees it. However, it all begins with a thought. That is why God urges you in His Word to keep your thoughts in line with His will. Be wary of the devil's attacks in the following areas.

## Lukewarmness

A very successful weapon that Satan often uses against the church is tempting believers to become *lukewarm*. In Revelation 3:15-16 (NASB) Jesus said:

**'I know your deeds, that you are neither cold nor hot; I would that you were cold or hot.**

**'So because you are lukewarm, and neither hot nor cold, I will spit you out of My mouth.'**

It is a trick of the enemy to get us to be wishy-washy, fence-walking Christians. When we are lukewarm, we have no authority or power; we lose our effectiveness in our own lives and in our family members' lives.

Lukewarmness is setting in if your relationship is not as "on fire" as when you first believed in the Lord Jesus Christ. You can reverse lukewarmness in your life by repenting and praying, "Dear Father, today I turn from my own ways. I turn toward You, God. I give You complete rulership in my life. Jesus is truly going to be Lord of my life."

Then, make Him Lord every day of your life. When you first wake up each morning, say, "I can choose today to either serve God, serve myself, or serve the devil. I choose to put on the Lord Jesus Christ. Not my will be done, but Your will shall be done in my life this day. Give me this day my daily bread."

You must make this decision daily. It is a daily walk. Today make a choice that Jesus will be Lord of every area of your life.

## Constant Temptation to Sin

Satan continually tries to *tempt you to sin*. His strategy is always the same. He knows that if he can get you — a believer — constantly dabbling in sin, you will become re-entangled in bondage. Then you will have no authority. Galatians 5:1 says:

**Stand fast...in the liberty wherewith Christ hath made us free, and be not entangled again with the yoke of bondage.**

The Body of Christ has not taken back very much territory, because many are under the same bondages of the world. (Remember the statistics I quoted in a previous chapter?) The Body of Christ has lost its savor or potency. This should not be so. We have been called out of darkness into light to make a difference in the world, but we first must *be* different.

I believe that you *are* making a difference in the world. Continue on! Your heart must long for this, or you would not have a desire to read this book. You don't have to become re-entangled with the bondage or yoke of the enemy. You don't have to submit to temptation.

I Corinthians 10:13 promises that God will provide a way out of temptation. Look for that way of escape when Satan tempts you. God always provides it. His Word is always true.

## Negative Thoughts

Satan creates strongholds in the lives of many women through a very cunning weapon: *negative thoughts* such as worry, doubt, discouragement, depression, condemnation, and fear.

Many women are living in despair because of the attack of the enemy on their minds. If this is true of you, I believe you are going to be set free from the enemy's clutches today in Jesus' Name. I really believe that.

Fear plagues many Christian women. They accept it as a ''normal'' emotion. II Timothy 1:7 says:

**God hath not given us the spirit of fear; but of power, and of love, and of a sound mind.**

The Lord audibly called out my name in my bedroom in August of 1989 to let me know that He is my protection and that He knows me by name.

You do not have to be afraid. When the Lord is your protection, nobody can harm you. However, when you are on your own, you have a lot to worry about.

- Psalm 32:7 (NIV) says, ''You are my hiding place; you will protect me from trouble and surround me with songs of deliverance.''

- In Exodus 33:17 (NIV), God said to Moses: ''…I will do the very thing you have asked, because I am pleased with you and I know you by name.'' So you do not have to be afraid.

- When fear of provision for the future hits you, remember what Jesus promised in Luke 12:7, ''But even the very hairs of your head are all numbered. Fear not therefore: ye are of more value than many sparrows.''

When you feel fear coming, read Psalm 46:1-2 and Psalm 91. The devil attacks your mind with these weapons to try to prevent you from receiving everything that God has for you and wants you to be. You don't have to receive negative thoughts. It is *your* choice. The Bible says:

**Finally, brethren, whatsoever things are true, whatsoever things are honest, whatsoever things are just, whatsoever things are pure, whatsoever things are lovely, whatsoever things are of good report; if there be any virtue [Do you want to be**

**a virtuous woman?], and if there be any praise, think on these things.**

**Philippians 4:8**

Do you know what this means? If, for example, you are listening to something that is not edifying, say, ''Excuse me. I have to go.'' Walk away from the conversation. If you are in your home watching television, turn it off when a program comes on that is immoral, indecent, and ungodly.

If you are at a theater, and the movie is full of curse words, you don't have to sit there and listen to it. Get up and walk out. That is okay to do. Yes, you may have paid $5 or $6 for each ticket, but it's not worth it to fill your mind with garbage. Remember, ''Garbage In, Garbage Out.'' (Even movies rated ''PG'' can be like this, so be careful.)

The Bible says, ''…Out of the abundance of the heart the mouth speaketh'' (Matthew 12:34). You must guard your mind from every thought that is contrary to the Word of God. If a negative thought comes, immediately attack back with the Word. Personalize it to your situation and say the Word out loud:

**I cast down this imagination. I cast down this thought that is contrary to the Word and that is trying to lift itself up against the Word and the knowledge of God. I take that thought captive and make it obedient to Christ. I cast it down and I will not accept it (II Corinthians 10:5).**

Do you know what happens to that thought when you do this? It leaves. There is power in the Word.

**What you think is what you say.
What you say is what you get.**

An excellent example of this is found in Numbers 13:33, ''And there we saw the giants...and we were in our own sight as grasshoppers, and so we were in their sight.'' How you see yourself is exactly how the enemy sees you.

Remember, Proverbs 23:7 says, ''For as he thinketh in his heart, so is he....'' If you think you are weak, you are! It is critical that you see yourself the way God sees you — in Christ Jesus! This is a life-or-death decision. If you don't see yourself in Jesus, you will be powerless to stop the stealing, killing, and destruction of the devil in your life.

Stop listening and molding yourself into the image of the world, and start seeing yourself the way God sees you. He sees you righteous. He sees you perfect. He sees you as a member of His glorious church — without spot or wrinkle. Quit trying to tell God about your shortcomings and faults. Do you know why I say that? God cannot see your weaknesses, because He sees you through Jesus, who stands in front of you. God sees Jesus when He looks at you.

Quit letting the enemy put you down. Condemnation is not of God. If you are a true child of God, you will sense conviction from time to time when you have sinned. However, there is a big difference between conviction and condemnation. It is the enemy who brings condemnation.

You can recognize the difference between *conviction* and *condemnation* by a simple test. Ask yourself the following questions.

1. Do I feel *drawn to* the Lord to receive forgiveness? If so, this is *conviction*. This is the Holy Spirit endeavoring to bring you back into fellowship with your loving, merciful heavenly Father. He is wanting you to turn to God.

2. Do I feel like I am being *pulled away* or *separated* from the Lord, like I could never be good enough to

deserve His love? If so, this is *condemnation*. It is from the devil. The Holy Spirit will never try to convince you that you are unfit to turn to God. No human being will ever be fit; that's why your heavenly Father sent Jesus to die for you and for me. God's love and mercy through Jesus covers all your sins. When you feel condemned, immediately rebuke the devil and turn to Jesus for help.

The verb *convict* comes from the Latin word meaning "to overcome, conquer."[1] The purpose of conviction is to help you to overcome or to conquer your sin and the devil's work in your life.

On the other hand, *condemn* comes from Latin words meaning to doom, blame, and harm.[2] The devil's purpose in attempting to condemn you is to hurt you and to try to get you to choose separation from God. You do have a choice, though. *You can choose Jesus and receive eternal life, or you can turn away from Him and doom yourself to eternal death.* Only *you* have this choice; the devil can never make it for you.

## Accusations about Your Past Failures

The devil plagues many believers with *accusations about past failures*. This is a trick of the enemy. Satan uses this to try to cause you to stumble and pull away from God.

Your enemy is continually whispering in your ear, "You're such a miserable failure. You can't do anything." If you listen to his lies, the devil will trap you into thinking about your past failures so much that you do nothing with your life for God today.

---

[1] *Webster's New Universal Unabridged Dictionary*, ed. Jean L. McKechnie and others (New York: Simon and Schuster, 1983), p. 400.

[2] *Ibid.*, p. 379.

This is the only *today* you will ever have. Before you know it, *today* will quickly slip into *yesterday*. Make every moment of today count for the Lord, while you still can.

I want to declare this to you: everyone has failed. I have failed. Every speaker standing on a platform has failed and fallen short of the glory of God. This might come as a devastating blow to some Christians, but we must realize the truth. No one on this planet is perfect, except Jesus Christ, and who are we supposed to put our affection on? Who are we supposed to put on a pedestal? Jesus! Nobody else.

You should be nice and reverent to your pastor, pastor's wife, and all leadership; but you should never worship any human being. Many people have fallen into hero worship. **This is dangerous, because if the hero falls the people fall. Jesus Christ will never let you down. He will never fall.** He is your Perfect Hero. When you put your confidence and trust in Him, He will never fail you. He has never failed me — He *can't* fail.

God does not remember your failures. You might say, "Oh, but I've been divorced three times." Or, "I've done this horrible thing." Or, maybe "I've had an abortion."

(In fact, in places where I have spoken, approximately 60% of the women in the audiences have admitted to having had abortions. Perhaps when I wrote about abortion in an earlier chapter, your heart was gripped with guilt. You might have even been a Christian when you had the abortion.)

Maybe you have said to yourself, "I've done this. There's no way God can use me."

I am writing this to tell you: yes, there is! There is *no* sin more powerful than the blood of Jesus Christ. If you ask forgiveness, His blood will cleanse you from *anything* you have ever done or will ever do — even abortion, divorce, and anything else you can name. Give to God the sin that has been plaguing you from your past — from yesterday. Give it to God today, and pray a simple prayer like this:

**God, I cannot deal with this in my strength. I cannot do anything about it. Father, I give it to You. Make my life what You want it to be. Use me for Your glory. I give this to You. Cleanse me by the blood of Jesus Christ. Amen.**

When you do this, He will make you completely brand new.

**Therefore if any man be in Christ, he is a new creature: old things are passed away; behold, all things are become new.**

**II Corinthians 5:17**

Jesus paid the debt for your failures so *you* would not have to! All you have to do is ask for His forgiveness. That's it. When you do, God will never remember your failures again; neither should you — no matter what the lying enemy tries to say.

**As far as the east is from the west, so far hath he removed our transgressions from us.**

**Psalm 103:12**

All you have to do is ask for forgiveness, receive it, then tell the devil that he is a liar. That's it! God erases your failures from all records. The devil can never *legally* discuss them again.

Let him who steals steal no longer in your life (Ephesians 4:28). This is a new day. Even if you have wrecked your life, forget the past. You cannot do anything to change the PAST; but you *can* say, "Lord, I give You myself *TODAY*." Concentrate on today and what you can do for God now.

The Apostle Paul said:

**Brethren, I do not regard myself as having laid hold of it yet; but one thing I do: forgetting what lies behind and reaching forward to what lies ahead,**

**I press on toward the goal for the prize of the upward call of God in Christ Jesus."**

**Philippians 3:13-14 (NASB)**

Whenever the enemy tries to defeat you by bringing up your *past* failures, remind him of his *future!* Tell him that the blood of Jesus cleanses you from *all* sin. You are a blood-bought, blood-washed child of God. The Lord has wiped your sins away.

Many Christians do not understand this. They know that God forgave and forgot their failures before they were saved. However, when they became Christians, they thought God began to keep a tally. After they fail to measure up, they think God will say at a certain point, "You're out of here." They feel justified in criticizing and condemning others, because *they* feel condemned.

God is faithful and just to forgive you and cleanse you (I John 1:9). Forget those things which are behind, but press on toward the future (Philippians 3:13-14). If you do not forget what is behind in your life — good and bad — then you cannot press forward. You will be trying to drive by looking in the rear-view mirror. It will not work.

Recently, the Lord showed me an important revelation. Normally when I think of Jesus, I either see Him sitting on a huge throne, or standing with His arms outstretched towards me as I walk toward Him.

One time, however, when I was worshipping the Lord, I had a vision of Him on the cross; I was standing at His feet. Suddenly a drop of His blood hit me. Blood began to cover me from head to toe as I stood at the feet of Jesus. (Normally, I am very squeamish and do not think this way.) Instantly that blood turned white as snow on my skin. It became transparent. My skin was brand new, like a baby's skin. There was no mark, blemish, or imperfection visible — everything was new!

God showed me that you and I as believers are covered with the blood of Jesus Christ. When He looks at us, He sees His Son's blood. Nothing you have done and nothing you will ever do is more powerful than that blood. It will never, ever lose its *POWER.*

You need to accept that today. Realize that you are forgiven and cleansed by His blood if you have accepted Jesus into your life. You are truly set free. So don't listen to the devil's lies. Don't let him hinder you any longer.

It is time that we take back those areas that the devil has stolen, killed, and destroyed. Through the Proclamation at the end of this book (see Appendix B), you will have an opportunity to tear down the enemy strongholds we have discussed in these two chapters. When you declare those words, I believe you will see God's power break the chains off your life.

# Part III
# What Are Your Capabilities?

# 7
# Unleash the Supernatural Strength of Your Forces

It is imperative that you know who is fighting on your side. As in physical war, you must know the power and strength of your allies in spiritual war.

## God Is on Your Side

The most important force you have on your side is God. Romans 8:31 (TLB) says, ''…If God is on our side, who can ever be against us?'' In Psalm 91:15, God promises to deliver you:

**He [that's you] shall call upon me, and I will answer him: I will be with him in trouble; I will deliver him, and honour him.**

The enemy knows that if he can tempt believers to sin, they will feel condemned and alienated from God. They won't have the confidence to call upon Him. They will start thinking they are not good enough to ask for the Lord's help, so they will stop calling out His Name and praying about the areas of attack, saying, ''I'll clean up my act, and *then* I'll get right with God.''

No! You must come to the Lord as you are today. He loved you as a sinner before you accepted Him into your life. Think how much more He loves you now that you are His child.

Have you lost some battles? Have you fallen down in some situations that you have been battling? So have I. Join the human race! Everyone has fallen down at one time or another; but the Lord is right there to pick you up and hold your hand, if you will only take His hand. Wherever there is a battle in your life — even if you have fallen down — God wants to turn it around for your good.

**And we know that God causes all things to work together for good to those who love God, to those who are called according to His purpose.**

**Romans 8:28 (NASB)**

Zechariah 4:6 (TLB) says, ''...This is God's message...'Not by might, nor by power, but by my Spirit, says the Lord of Hosts — you will succeed because of my Spirit, though you are few and weak.' ''

## Call upon the Angels

When Satan fell, two-thirds of the angelic hosts stayed in Heaven (II Peter 2:4, Revelation 12:1-11, Ezekiel 28:12-19). Do you realize what that means? One-third of God's former supernatural forces are with Satan, but two-thirds are with us!

One of the greatest stories in the Bible that illustrates this fact is in II Kings 6:14-17 (NASB). The enemy king of Syria had sent a great army to capture the Prophet Elisha. They came at night and surrounded the city where Elisha was. When Elisha's servant woke up early the next morning, he saw this horrifying, mighty army with horses and chariots, circling the city. He looked at his master and asked, ''What shall we do?''

Have *you* looked at a circumstance that is facing your life and asked, ''What shall we do?''

Elisha answered, "Do not fear, for those who are with us are more than those who are with the enemy." Then what did Elijah do? He prayed. "Dear God," he said, "let my servant see. Open his eyes and let him see." The Lord answered his prayer and opened the servant's eyes. He saw the mountain full of the supernatural forces of God all around Elisha. The Bible calls them "horses and chariots of fire."

We need to say, "Lord, open my eyes that I can see that we are truly surrounded by a great cloud of witnesses. There is more that are with us than with the enemy." We must realize that as believers, we have angels posted around us. Our forces are mighty in battle.

Hebrews 1:14 (TLB) says, "...For the angels are only spirit-messengers sent out to help and care for those who are to receive his salvation." The angels are here to help you, the believer.

They are also your protectors. Psalm 91:10-12 (TLB) promises this:

**How then can evil overtake me or any plague come near?**

**For he orders his angels to protect you wherever you go.**

**They will steady you with their hands to keep you from stumbling against the rocks on the trail [or on the road of life!]**

God sends them to protect you. Understand that I am not advocating the worship of angels. I merely want you to realize that they are here to help you whenever you need it. They are not little cherubs that you often see in religious art; but huge, powerful beings. Call upon them whenever you need supernatural protection or service.

Sometimes my son, Lance, is afraid to go to sleep at night. When this happens, I point to the poster on his wall and say, "See those Power Team guys with those swords? Angels are three times bigger than that, and they're standing right at the foot of your bed to protect you. Do you need to be afraid?"

"No," he answers.

"Why?" I ask.

"Because there's a big angel standing right there," he says, pointing to the foot of his bed. He believes it, and we need to believe it too.

## Join Your Faith With Fellow Believers

Not only do you have supernatural forces available to help you fight, but you have fellow believers here on earth to join forces with you. Don't let Satan catch you without prayer partners.

Remember, I Peter 5:8 (NASB) tells us that Satan is looking for people to devour, "...Your adversary, the devil, prowls about like a roaring lion, seeking someone to devour." Many times when an animal is stalking its prey, it waits for the one that wanders off alone. When that one is separated from the rest of the pack, the predator attacks. There is power in unity.

It's time that we know the enemy's devices. It's time that we wake up. Awake, oh church, you who slumber. Wake up; realize what time it is. It's time to say, "No more. No more will you rob in my life."

In Deuteronomy 32:30, the Bible says that one will chase 1,000 and two will put 10,000 to flight. (See also Joshua 23:10). Do you realize the multiplicative impact of adding merely a second believer in prayer? According to this

*Unleash the Supernatural Strength of Your Forces*

Scripture you increase your power by 1,000%! Each person becomes five times more powerful than when praying alone.

Now can you understand why marriages are especially under such great attack? The enemy does not want husbands and wives to be in agreement. When the unity of a marriage is disrupted, the power to do warfare against the enemy is thwarted.

The devil knows that the unity of a married couple is a powerfully destructive force against his works. **He knows that together you and your husband in the Name of Jesus can put the demons to flight that are coming to destroy your finances, your business, your lives, your family, your destiny, and your future in God.**

He is trying to destroy your marriage first so you will lose your power to defeat him. Don't listen to his attacks on your mind in this area. Stay in agreement and in prayer with your husband. Jesus said:

**Again I say unto you, That if two of you shall agree on earth as touching any thing that they shall ask, it shall be done for them of my Father which is in heaven.**

**Matthew 18:19**

Determine to be a team player. Ecclesiastes 4:9-12 says that two are better than one because if one falls or is attacked, the other can help. When you are under attack, get your husband or a fellow believer — a prayer warrior — to pray with you.

You are hindered and virtually ineffective against the enemy when the bond of unity is broken. Remember, the enemy's strategy is always to divide and conquer.

**And Jesus knew their thoughts, and said unto them, Every kingdom divided against itself is**

**brought to desolation; and every city or house divided against itself shall not stand....**

**Matthew 12:25**

**Now I beseech you, brethren, by the name of our Lord Jesus Christ, that ye all speak the same thing, and that there be no divisions among you; but that ye be perfectly joined together in the same mind and in the same judgment.**

**I Corinthians 1:10**

If you are single, you can still have great power when you join together with another believer or with many believers in your local church. Leviticus 26:8 says, "And five of you shall chase an hundred, and an hundred of you shall put ten thousand to flight: and your enemies shall fall before you by the sword." I believe that is the Sword of the Spirit, the Word of God. (We will discuss this in detail in the next chapter.)

Now do you see why the devil does not want people in church? Their power multiplies phenomenally when they join together with other believers. Do you realize that in a local church, for example, the collective power of 100 versus five believers is increased by 10,000% according to this Scripture? Again, each person becomes five times more powerful when joined together with other believers.

The enemy knows that where two or more are gathered in Jesus' Name, the Lord is in their midst (Matthew 18:20). There is strength in unity. Satan knows what a powerful, city-changing force a united local church can be.

That is why he tries to cause division, strife, and criticism in churches that are preparing to take regions and cities for God. Division and strife are not of God. Remember, what is the sign of warfare? Strife, division, confusion. These are of the devil.

*Unleash the Supernatural Strength of Your Forces*

He sidetracks Christians by getting us to fight *one another* over petty matters, so we won't fight the *real* enemy, him! It's time that we stop shadow boxing. The devil knows that when we are fighting one another, we are rarely evangelistic.

This is why I believe we have not reached the world with the Gospel. *Evangelism* should be our major battlefront. We need to spend our energy pulling the captives out of the clutches of the enemy into life. Jesus, our example, described our mission when He spoke about Himself:

**The Spirit of the Lord is upon me [and you], because he hath anointed me [and you] to preach the gospel to the poor; he hath sent me [and you] to heal the brokenhearted, to preach deliverance to the captives, and recovering of sight to the blind, to set at liberty them that are bruised,**

**To preach the acceptable year of the Lord.**

**Luke 4:18-19**

This is true for every one of us who is a believer. God has anointed us to evangelize the world. We must have a heart for souls like Jesus did. When we win a soul to Christ, we are truly helping bring sight to the blind — light to those who are in darkness. Evangelism is the heartbeat of God.

If you ever hear or see anything that is attempting to distract from the power of the Gospel or the unity, love, and peace in the Body of Christ, you need to pray. Ask God to come into that situation like a flood.

Are *you* involved with God in what He is building? Or do you want God to be a part of what you are building? If you have missed His will, repent and get back into right fellowship with other believers in a local church.

When you are joined to the family of God in a local church, you are joined to one of the most powerful influences in the world today. The local church is a God-ordained institution. In Matthew 16:18, Jesus said:

> **And I say also unto thee, That thou art Peter, and upon this rock I will build my church; and the gates of hell shall not prevail against it.**

Be a committed member of a local church. If you are single, the leadership will be your spiritual head (umbrella of protection). I don't mean this in an extreme way, but in a balanced, biblical way. Hebrews 13:17 says, "...For they watch for your souls, as they that must give account...."

I believe that the only way we are going to survive in this decade is to unite. The Body of Christ must have one mind, making every effort to keep the unity of the Spirit through the bond of peace. Then the peace of God that passes all understanding will guard your *heart* and your *mind* through Christ Jesus.

Do you need peace in your life? Then you need to *keep peace*. It begins with you — in your home with your husband, children, or parents. Yes, it takes effort to keep peace, but the resulting power of unity is worth it!

Do you know the best way to keep peace? Bite your tongue.

> **A soft answer turneth away wrath: but grievous words stir up anger.**
>
> **Proverbs 15:1**

If you make this effort, then the peace of God that passes all understanding will guard your heart and your mind through Christ Jesus (Philippians 4:7). I challenge you today to pray for the restoration of unity and peace in the

*Unleash the Supernatural Strength of Your Forces*

Body of Christ. Be a part of the solution. Help the Body of Christ exercise her God-given power.

Don't let the enemy divide in your life. Stay in unity with your fellow Christians and everyone around you so you can significantly enhance your power to battle the enemy!

Remember, as you pray with fellow believers, you can call upon the angels for supernatural help in times of trouble. God is truly on your side. Nothing can stand against you when you pray in unity with your brothers and sisters in Christ.

# 8
# Pick up Your Weapons of Power

You have powerful weapons to defeat every enemy onslaught. When you recognize an attack on your life or on your family, stop and declare, "Wait a minute! This attack will not succeed against my family and me, because greater is He that is in me than he that is in the world. This attack will not prosper. It will not overtake my life in Jesus' Name."

Remember II Corinthians 10:3-5 (NASB) says:

> **For though we walk in the flesh, we do not war according to the flesh,**
>
> **for the weapons of our warfare are not of the *flesh* [KJV says *carnal*], but divinely powerful for the destruction of fortresses.**
>
> **We are destroying speculations and every lofty thing raised up against the knowledge of God, and we are taking every thought captive to the obedience of Christ.**

The Greek word for *carnal* is *sarkikos*, (sar-kee-kos') which implies human weakness;[1] and the Greek word for *flesh*, *sarx*, (sarx) refers to "the natural attainments of men."[2]

---

[1] W.E. Vine, M.A., *Vine's Expository Dictionary of New Testament Words* (Peabody: Hendrickson Publishers, Unabridged Edition), pp. 171, 448.

[2] *Ibid.*, p. 448.

Verse 4 in *The Living Bible* says, ''I use God's mighty weapons, not those made by men, to knock down the devil's strongholds.'' Your weapons are not limited to the abilities of man, but have supernatural power!

## The Armor of God

Every morning without fail, you must pick up your weapons against the devil. Put on the armor of God as described in Ephesians 6:10-13 (NASB):

**Finally, be strong in the Lord, and in the strength of His might.**

**Put on the full armor of God, that you may be able to stand firm against the schemes of the devil.**

**For our struggle is not against flesh and blood, but against the rulers, against the powers, against the world forces of darkness, against spiritual forces of wickedness in heavenly places.**

**Therefore, take up the full armor of God, that you may be able to resist in the evil day, and having done everything, to stand firm.**

The Phillips translation says, ''...that even when you have fought to a standstill you may stand your ground.'' Do you feel like you are at a standstill in your Christian walk? Verses 14-18 (NASB) contain your answer:

**Stand firm therefore, having** *girded your loins with truth,* **and having put on the** *breastplate of righteousness,*

**and having** *shod your feet with the preparation of the Gospel of peace;*

**in addition to all, taking up the** *shield of faith* **with which you will be able to extinguish all the flaming missiles of the evil one.**

**And take the *helmet of salvation*, and the *sword of the Spirit*, which is the word of God.**

**With all prayer and petition pray at all times in the Spirit, and with this in view, be on the alert with all perseverance and petition for all the saints.**

*Girdle of Truth*

The first part of your armor is the *Girdle of Truth*. In the Bible, soldiers *girded up their loins* in preparation for natural war. They wore military girdles, from which swords or daggers were suspended.[3]

*Loins* in the Greek is *osphus* (os-foos'). In this Scripture about the armor of God, it means, "bracing up oneself so as to maintain perfect sincerity and reality as the counteractive in Christian character against hypocrisy and falsehood."[4]

Why does the Bible call this the Girdle of Truth? The Greek word for *truth* here is *aletheuo* (al-ayth-yoo'-o), meaning "to deal faithfully or truly with anyone."[5]

I Peter 1:13-16 says:

**Wherefore gird up the *loins of your mind*, be sober, and hope to the end for the grace that is to be brought unto you at the revelation of Jesus Christ;**

**As obedient children, not fashioning yourselves according to the former lusts in your ignorance:**

---

[3] *Smith's Bible Dictionary* (Westwood: Barbour Books, 1987), p. 215.
[4] Vine, p. 692.
[5] *Ibid.*, p. 1182.

**But as he which hath called you is holy, so be ye holy in all manner of conversation;**

**Because it is written, Be ye holy; for I am holy.**

Daily you must prepare yourself for battle by girding or bracing up your mind with Truth. Who is Truth? Jesus is Truth. Put on the mind of Christ every day (I Corinthians 2:16).

Speak and act in all your ways in the holiness of Truth. Before you can be successful in battle, you must first make a commitment to God's way of life: Truth.

*Breastplate of Righteousness*

God brought righteousness through His Son, Jesus.

**And He [God] saw that there was no man,**

**And was astonished that there was no one to intercede;**

**Then His own arm brought salvation to Him;**

**And His righteousness upheld Him.**

**And He put on righteousness like a breastplate,**

**And a helmet of salvation on His head;**

**And He put on garments of vengeance for clothing,**

**And wrapped Himself with zeal as a mantle.**

**"And a Redeemer will come to Zion,**

**And to those who turn from transgression in Jacob," declares the Lord.**

**Isaiah 59:16, 17, 20 (NASB)**

What is righteousness? It is right standing with God; a gift to all who believe in Christ's finished work at Calvary.

How do you stay in right standing with God? Daily ask for His cleansing forgiveness through the blood of Jesus, and thank Him for what He has done in your life. Daily say, "I can do nothing except by Your strength, Lord. You are the One who empowers me. You are my righteousness. Create a clean heart in me, Lord."

In the natural wars of the Bible, the breastplate protected "the body on both sides, from the neck to the middle."[6] It fortified the vital organs, especially the heart.

Spiritually, the righteousness of Christ is the Christian's breastplate. Right standing with God protects your heart and keeps it pure, enabling you to stand against the enemy's attacks, because "if our hearts do not condemn us, we have confidence before God..." (I John 3:21, NIV).

To be victorious against the enemy, you must have a clean heart as Jesus did. Because of His righteousness, Jesus said that the devil had no claim on Him (John 14:30). David recognized the importance of a clean heart, when he prayed in Psalm 51:10-12, "Create in me a clean heart, O God...."

You need to ask the Lord daily to cleanse you so you are not tainted by the world and the ruler of this world. Each day, put on the Breastplate of Righteousness. Stay in rightstanding with God through the righteousness of Jesus.

When your heart is pure before the Lord, joy will overtake you, bringing you strength.

> **...Do not be grieved, for the joy of the Lord is your strength.**
>
> **Nehemiah 8:10 (NASB)**

---

[6]*Ibid.*, p. 151.

When you are depressed you have lost confidence in God, and your strength has fled. Don't let the enemy steal your joy; because when he has your joy, he has your power.

To keep your heart pure and full of joy, daily declare the righteousness and faithfulness of God. When you speak the Word to the devil, you render him helpless and you empower yourself with the strength of God. Begin to confess the Word when you feel the devil is trying to steal your joy.

- I rejoice in the Lord always (Philippians 4:4).
- I can do all things through Christ who strengthens me (Philippians 4:13).
- Greater is He that is in me, than he that is in the world (I John 4:4).
- In all these things I am more than a conqueror through Christ. For I am persuaded, that neither death, nor life, nor angels, nor principalities, nor powers, nor things present, nor things to come, nor height, nor depth, nor any other creature, shall be able to separate me from the love of God, which is in Christ Jesus my Lord (Romans 8:37-39).

Stand firmly in the righteousness of Jesus each day. Don't allow the enemy to sway you from your glorious Protector. (For more Scriptures, turn to Appendix C.)

### *Feet Shod with the Preparation of the Gospel of Peace*

The feet were covered with shoes of brass, in biblical times of natural war, to protect a marching army against dangerous ground traps laid by the enemy.[7]

---

[7]Matthew Henry, *Commentary on the Whole Bible,* (Grand Rapids: Zondervan Publishing House, 1961), p. 1858.

*Pick up Your Weapons of Power*

In spiritual war, you are to cover your feet with the preparation of the Gospel of peace. *Preparation* in the Greek is *hetoimasia* (het-oy-mas-ee'-ah), which means "readiness" or "firm footing (foundation)."[8]

"...The Gospel itself is to be the firm footing of the believer, his walk being worthy of it and therefore a testimony in regard to it."[9]

This is the Gospel of Peace. In the Greek, *peace* here is *eirene* (i-ray'-nay). It implies prosperity: peace, quietness, rest; it means to set at one again.[10] This refers to "the tranquil state of a soul assured of its salvation through Christ...."[11]

No matter what traps the enemy sets before you, as you march forward in God's army, the Gospel of Peace is your firm footing. You can rest assured that God will prosper you and put all the pieces back together again.

Your life should be a testimony of the Gospel of Peace. Spread peace wherever you go, not discord. Share good news, not bad news. Talk more about the good things God has done in your life, rather than how bad things are. Isaiah 52:7 (NASB) says:

> **How lovely on the mountains**
> **Are the feet of him who brings good news,**
> **Who announces peace**
> **And brings good news of happiness,**
> **Who announces salvation,**
> **And says to Zion, "Your God reigns!"**

---

[8]Vine, p. 886.

[9]*Ibid.*

[10]James Strong, LL.D., S.T.D., *The New Strong's Exhaustive Concordance of the Bible* (Nashville: Thomas Nelson Publishers, 1984), p. 25.

[11]Joseph Henry Thayer, D.D., *Thayer's Greek-English Lexicon of the New Testament* (Marshallton: The National Foundation for Christian Education), p. 182.

### *Shield of Faith*

In the natural wars of the Bible, this particular kind of shield was large and oblong. It protected the whole body of the soldier, because it could be turned in any direction.[12] Shields protected the armies of God's children against the literal flaming, fire-tipped,[13] poisonous darts flung by the enemy.[14]

In spiritual war, your faith or belief is like a shield, "a sort of universal defence."[15] As a believer, you can turn your faith in the direction the enemy is attacking, and it will "extinguish all the flaming missiles of the evil one" (NASB). That's what faith will do for you.

What exactly is faith? Hebrews 11:1 says, "Now faith is the substance of things hoped for, the evidence of things not seen." In the Greek, the word for *faith* is *pistis* (pis'-tis), which is defined as "firm persuasion, a conviction based upon hearing."[16]

Romans 10:17 reiterates this by stating that faith comes by hearing (and by hearing the Word of God). In contrast then, *unbelief* also must come by hearing the thoughts of the enemy. (You can recognize his thoughts as any which are contrary to the Word.)

Another definition for *faith* is "reliance upon Christ for salvation."[17] Faith is your belief that God can save you no matter what, that He is powerful enough to do the impossible. It is believing that God really is God. Faith is

---

[12]Vine, p. 1045.

[13]*Ibid.*, p. 433.

[14]Henry, p. 1858.

[15]*Ibid.*

[16]Vine, p. 411.

[17]Strong, p. 58.

*Pick up Your Weapons of Power*

"constancy in such profession."[18] Faith does not waver by circumstances. Hebrews 10:23 says:

**Let us hold fast the profession of our faith without wavering; (for he is faithful that promised).**

By faith, you as a believer can see reality as God sees it — not as the devil is trying to make you think it is. Hebrews 11:1 (AMP) says:

**Now faith is the assurance (the confirmation, the title-deed) of the things [we] hope for, being the proof of things [we] do not see and the conviction of their reality — faith perceiving as real fact what is not revealed to the senses.**

I want you to hear this: without faith it is impossible to please God (Hebrews 11:6). You must daily renew your faith in Him, because there is no other worthy of your faith — not even yourself.

**...Contend earnestly for the faith which was once for all delivered to the saints.**

**Jude 1:3 (NASB)**

**For whatsoever is born of God overcometh the world: and this is the victory that overcometh the world, even our faith.**

**I John 5:4**

You must determine that no matter what happens, you will *believe the Lord and His Word*. You must believe this *more* than what you see with your natural eyes.

**But when he [that's you] asks, he must *believe* and *not doubt*, because he who doubts is like a wave of the sea, blown and tossed by the wind.**

---
[18]*Ibid.*

**That man should not think he will receive anything from the Lord;**

**he is a double-minded man, unstable in all he does."**

*James 1:6-8 (NIV)*

You have to be strong to do battle. The enemy's strategies are always the same. He wants to keep you a weak, ineffective, wishy-washy Christian.

You must use your Shield of Faith as protection against the fiery darts of doubt that Satan throws at your mind. His plan is to bring in doubt, which will hinder your prayers and break your power. You cannot afford to doubt.

Do you have an area in your life that you must have an answer for? Maybe it is your finances, children, marriage, career, or your health. Stop looking at the problem, and get your eyes fixed on the solution: Jesus Christ. Nothing is impossible with God. Remember James 4:7 (NASB), which says, "Submit therefore to God. Resist the devil and he will flee from you."

In order to overcome the enemy, you must be determined to be:

- Firm in faith
- Rooted
- Established
- Strong
- Immoveable

When you do, you will begin to see the enemy and his confusion and strife flee from your life.

*Helmet of Salvation*

In Bible times, the helmet protected a soldier's head and brain, an extremely vital and vulnerable part of the body.

Spiritually, the Helmet of Salvation protects or *defends* the believer against eternal death and his or her mind against the enemy's attacks.

*Salvation* in the Greek is *soterion* (so-tay'-ree-on), meaning defender or defence. It is a form of the word for *savior*.[19] Our hope is in Christ (I Timothy 1:1).

The moment you first believed in Christ, you put on the Helmet of Salvation. You became a brand-new creation in Christ Jesus (II Corinthians 5:17). You took on the mind of Christ and eternal life.

> **...As many as received Him, to them He gave the right to become children of God...."**
>
> **John 1:12 (NASB)**
>
> **For by grace you have been saved through faith; and that not of yourselves, it is the gift of God;**
>
> **not as a result of works, that no one should boast."**
>
> **Ephesians 2:8-9 (NASB)**

The Helmet of Salvation is also a spirit of grace rather than condemnation. Romans 8:1 (NASB) says, "There is therefore now no condemnation for those who are in Christ Jesus."

Daily you need to gird up the loins of your mind. Daily put on the Helmet of Salvation and put on Truth in your

---

[19]*Ibid.*, p. 70.

mind. Then you can recognize the enemy's flaming missiles of wrong thinking.

The devil is trying to get you to think like the world does. That's why 23% of the Christian households hooked into cable television have pornographic channels in their homes — the same percentage as the world. The enemy has gradually polluted their thinking.

Daily, you must gird up your mind. Spiritual warfare is a *daily* event. When the enemy tempts you to think wrongly, remember the verse quoted earlier:

> **Finally, brethren, whatsoever things are true, whatsoever things are honest, whatsoever things are just, whatsoever things are pure, whatsoever things are lovely, whatsoever things are of good report; if there be any virtue, and if there be any praise, think on these things.**
>
> **Philippians 4:8**

*The Sword of the Spirit*

*Sword* in the Greek is *machaira* (makh'-ahee-rah), meaning "a weapon...used for war, or for quarrels and dissensions that destroy peace...."[20] This weapon was used in the Bible to restore peace in the natural realm.

Similarly in the spiritual realm, the Sword of the Spirit, or the Word of God, is the weapon you should use to speak peace back into any unruly situation. (Do not use the Word to argue or fight!) Do you remember how Jesus calmed the storm when He and His disciples were about to sink in the boat?

> **And he arose, and rebuked the wind, and said unto the sea, Peace, be still. And the wind ceased, and there was a great calm.**
>
> **Mark 4:39**

---

[20]Thayer, p. 393.

**Verily I say unto you, Whatsoever ye shall bind on earth shall be bound in heaven: and whatsoever ye shall loose on earth shall be loosed in heaven.**

**Matthew 18:18**

The words you speak are extremely powerful. Proverbs 18:21 says that death and life are in the power of the tongue. It is difficult to admit the truth, but the Bible singles out women for the problems our tongues cause. There is a reason for this. If used correctly, think about the power of life that we as women can bring to every area of our lives. We must speak God's Word (truth and life) — not the devil's lies (death).

Remember this. The Bible says, ''And they overcame him by the blood of the Lamb, and by the WORD of their testimony...'' (Revelation 12:11). Do you want to be an overcomer in every circumstance of life? This Scripture explains the two reasons that you overcome and have victory in your life:

- The forgiveness and redemption Jesus bought for you
- The words you speak from your mouth; your testimony

The Body of Christ understands the redemptive work of Jesus at Calvary. However, how many Christians realize that the words they speak can bring death or life, defeat or victory?

In the past, I thought that Satan knew my thoughts; but I want you to know that he does not know what you are thinking. He can tempt you with evil thoughts, but he does not know if you have received them until you speak. The enemy only knows that you are weak by the words that come out of your mouth. He can only know that he is getting to you, if you speak it; so watch what comes out of your mouth.

The Sword of the Spirit is your only *offensive* weapon in the armor! Pray the Word over yourself and your family daily. Be on the offensive. Stop the devil before He attacks.

Remember that the Word is the will of God. It is important to see yourself as God sees you in Christ Jesus! Then speak it into all areas of your life.

At the end of this book in Appendix C, you will find many Scriptures to speak and pray over your life, your husband, your children, your lost loved ones, your pastor, and the nation. Feel free to add any others that particularly fit your situation. Then, daily pray these over your life. If you ever feel weak and don't think you have any strength to pray, get this book out and pray those Scriptures.

One of the main purposes of Satan is to devour the Word from your heart. He wants to steal the Sword of the Spirit, the Word of God, from you. In Matthew 13:3-4 (NKJV) Jesus told the parable of the sower:

> ..."**Behold, a sower went out to sow.**
>
> "**And as he sowed, some seed fell by the wayside; and the birds came and devoured them....**"

Jesus explained the meaning of the parable in verse 19:

> "**When anyone hears the word of the kingdom, and does not understand [or comprehend] it, then the wicked one [Satan] comes and snatches away what was sown in his heart....**"

One of the most powerful weapons that you have as a Christian is the Word of God. This is why Satan is constantly trying to steal the Word from you. Attempting to instill doubt, he questions you, ''Did God really say that to you? Did He really give you that promise?''

When Satan tempted Jesus in the desert, what did Jesus use to combat him? He used the Word of God. The same enemy is trying the same strategy on you: he wants to snatch the Word of God out of your heart. He wants to take away your weapons so you will be powerless against him.

Remember Romans 10:17 says, ''So then faith cometh by hearing, and hearing by the word of God.'' When that Word is stolen from your heart, you don't have faith. You don't have confidence to move that mountain — that area that is hindering your life. You must have faith if you are going to engage in spiritual warfare, or the enemy will devour you.

It is vitally important to guard the Word in your heart. When a thought comes that is contrary to the Word of God, stop and say, ''Wait a minute. I do not accept that. I do not accept it, because the Word says....'' Then quote a Scripture promise about that area.

Now you can only do this if you know the Word. Have you ever wondered why you could read any boring book and not fall asleep at night; but the moment you pick up your Bible, it is like you took the most powerful sedative there is? It is because the enemy does not want you to get the Word.

Remember, the Word of God is your offensive weaponry. It enables you to ''punch out the devil.'' It worked for Jesus when He was in conflict with Satan in the wilderness. It will work for you, because Jesus is the Supreme Example of how to fight spiritual warfare.

**Then was Jesus led up of the Spirit into the wilderness to be tempted of the devil.**

And when he had fasted forty days and forty nights, he was afterward an hungred.

And when the tempter came to him, he said, If thou be the Son of God, command that these stones be made bread.

But he answered and said, It is written, Man shall not live by bread alone, but by every word that proceedeth out of the mouth of God.

Then the devil taketh him up into the holy city, and setteth him on a pinnacle of the temple,

And saith unto him, If thou be the Son of God, cast thyself down: for it is written, He shall give his angels charge concerning thee: and in their hands they shall bear thee up, lest at any time thou dash thy foot against a stone.

Jesus said unto him, It is written again, Thou shalt not tempt the Lord thy God.

Again, the devil taketh him up into an exceeding high mountain, and sheweth him all the kingdoms of the world, and the glory of them;

And saith unto him, All these things will I give thee, if thou wilt fall down and worship me.

Then saith Jesus unto him, Get thee hence, Satan: for it is written, Thou shalt worship the Lord thy God, and him only shalt thou serve.

Then the devil leaveth him, and, behold, angels came and ministered unto him.

**Matthew 4:1-11**

You must believe that the Bible is the Word of God and that it is the ultimate authority over your life. To gain the attention of the ruling evil spirits, you simply say what God has already said. It worked for Jesus; it will work for you.

Praying the Word builds your confidence and keeps your faith focused, so you can receive what you need. When you pray in faith, you have the power to move any mountain. **Praying God's Word in every area of your life will empower you to reclaim the territory that the enemy has stolen from you.**

Has God given you a dream or a vision for your life that has not yet come to pass? Maybe you have "put it on the shelf," hoping that one day it *will* become reality.

Now is the time to pray the Word over that dream. Use this time to build your faith to receive the manifestation of your vision. Remember, "...he is a rewarder of them that diligently seek him" (Hebrews 11:6). Stay in faith, and don't stop until you see your vision come to pass.

## Don't Forget to Get Dressed Every Day!

You must remember to put on the Lord Jesus Christ daily. He is your armor. Walk in Him and in His strength. Then you will overcome *every* temptation of the enemy.

> **But put on the Lord Jesus Christ, and make no provision for the flesh, to fulfill its lusts.**
> **Romans 13:14 (NKJV)**

When you put on Jesus, you will make no provision for the flesh, because He is your Helmet of Salvation. He is your Breastplate of Righteousness. He is your Shield of Faith. He is Truth and the Sword of the Spirit, the Word of God. He is your Gospel of Peace. He is Peace.

Each morning, put Jesus first in your life. Receive the power of the blood and the stripes of Jesus for your forgiveness and healing.

Christians walk headlong into spiritual warfare when we walk away from the Lord, become influenced by the world, and begin thinking like the world.

Never forget: the world is constantly challenging the Word of God (like Satan did in the Garden of Eden with Eve). If there is a particular area of your life where the devil is continually attacking, here is what you should do as a believer:

1. **Equip yourself with the Word (Truth).** Get all the scriptural promises you can find. Feed your spirit man on the Word of God.

2. **Wage war against the devil and his lies.** Use the Truth as ammunition to bombard the enemy. Quote the Word about your situation back to him.

If you continue this without ceasing, you *will* see the power of God's Word set you free from the bondage of Satan.

**So shall my word be that goeth forth out of my mouth: it shall not return unto me *void*, but it shall accomplish that which I please, and it shall prosper in the thing whereto I sent it.**

**Isaiah 55:11**

The Word cannot return void. The definition of *void* in today's civil law is "of no legal force; not binding; invalid; null."[21] The Word has *legal power* and *will* accomplish what we send it to do.

Now, do you see why we as Christians are not always victorious in spiritual warfare? We have not had our armor on. We must put on the complete armor of God, so there

---

[21]*Webster's New Universal Unabridged Dictionary,* ed. Jean L. McKechnie and others (New York: Simon and Schuster, 1983), p. 2047.

will be no handles for the enemy to manipulate or to control us with. **Let's get dressed every day!**

# 9
# Overcome by the Power of the Spirit

An extremely powerful defensive weapon that you have as a believer is walking in the Spirit. Remember, the flesh is at war with the Spirit, and is an easy prey to the devil's attacks. However, you gain the advantage over your flesh (and the devil) by walking in the Spirit. The Bible is very clear about this.

> This I say then, Walk in the Spirit, and ye shall not fulfil the lust of the flesh.
>
> For the flesh lusteth against the Spirit, and the Spirit against the flesh: and these are contrary the one to the other: so that ye cannot do the things that ye would.
>
> But if ye be led of the Spirit, ye are not under the law.
>
> Now the works of the flesh are manifest, which are these; Adultery, fornication, uncleanness, lasciviousness,
>
> Idolatry, witchcraft, hatred, variance, emulations, wrath, strife, seditions, heresies,
>
> Envyings, murders, drunkenness, revellings, and such like: of the which I tell you before, as I have also told you in time past, that they which do such things shall not inherit the kingdom of God.

> But the fruit of the Spirit is love, joy, peace, longsuffering, gentleness, goodness, faith,
>
> Meekness, temperance: against such there is no law.
>
> And they that are Christ's have crucified the flesh with the affections and lusts.
>
> If we live in the Spirit, let us also walk in the Spirit.
>
> **Galatians 5:16-25**

Cultivate all the fruits of the Spirit in your life. Practice them daily, especially the first one listed, love.

## Walk in Love

*Love* is one of your major weapons against the onslaughts of the enemy. When you walk in love, you defeat the devil *before* he can create any strongholds in your life through his weapons of *conflict, hostility, and strife.*

Remember, James 3:16 says, "For where envying and strife is, there is confusion and every evil work." Love brings peace and power. Strife brings fear and evil.

> There is no fear in love; but perfect love casteth out fear: because fear hath torment. He that feareth is not made perfect in love.
>
> **I John 4:18**

When the enemy floods your home, your job, your church, or any area of your life with strife and conflict, here is what you should do. Let the love of God flow out of you to those who are around you. You *will* see changes happen. The Bible teaches us what love is.

> Though I speak with the tongues of men and of angels, but have not love, I have become as sounding brass or a clanging cymbal.
>
> And though I have the gift of prophecy, and understand all mysteries and all knowledge, and though I have all faith, so that I could remove mountains, but have not love, I am nothing.
>
> And though I bestow all my goods to feed the poor, and though I give my body to be burned, but have not love, it profits me nothing.
>
> Love suffers long and is kind; love does not envy; love does not parade itself, is not puffed up;
>
> does not behave rudely, does not seek its own, is not provoked, thinks no evil;
>
> does not rejoice in iniquity, but rejoices in the truth;
>
> *bears* all things, *believes* all things, *hopes* all things, *endures* all things.
>
> LOVE NEVER FAILS....
>
> And now abide faith, hope, love, these three; but the greatest of these is love.
>
> I Corinthians 13:1-8, 13 (NKJV)

Let love be the reason behind your every action. Who is Love? God is Love. Allow Him to guide you in loving the unlovely. It is a commandment that He has given you.

> If a man say, I love God, and hateth his brother, he is a liar: for he that loveth not his brother whom he hath seen, how can he love God whom he hath not seen?
>
> I John 4:20

> For all the law is fulfilled in one word, even in this; Thou shalt love thy neighbour as thyself.
>
> **Galatians 5:14**

## Become Lost in Service to Others

Another important weapon in spiritual warfare is to become lost in *service* to others.

> For you were called to freedom, brethren; only do not turn your freedom into an opportunity for the flesh, through love serve one another.
>
> **Galatians 5:13 (NASB)**

Recently on television I saw a Christian leader share an excellent testimony about depression. This person was so despondent, that nothing else seemed important. She was literally held captive in her own home and could not maintain a normal lifestyle.

One day, the Lord instructed her to pray for a particular person who was in a condition much worse than her. At first, she did not feel like praying. However, when she stepped out in obedience and prayed for this individual, this Christian leader found herself healed — completely set free!

This story is evidence of the truth found in a very powerful verse.

> ...Pray one for another, so that you may be healed. The effective prayer of a righteous man can accomplish much.
>
> **James 5:16 (NASB)**

Isn't that powerful? You find someone who needs help when you need help, and God will heal you. In other words, **when you *do* something for someone else, God does something for *you*.** Something happens in *your* life. This is opposite of natural thinking, but it works! It is a promise from the Word of God.

If you grasp this and apply it in your life, you will see many changes. No longer will you be angry when you have to do something for your husband or pick up after the children. This will keep you from focusing only on yourself and your needs.

If there is a certain area of your life where you need help, ask the Lord to show you someone who needs help. Then put that person's needs first. When you do, God will meet your needs. When you esteem others more highly than yourself, He will meet your needs every time.

## Be Faithful

A powerful weapon many Christians overlook is *faithfulness.* Faithfulness in the few things prepares you to rule over much.

> **His lord said unto him, Well done, thou good and faithful servant: thou hast been faithful over a few things, I will make thee ruler over many things: enter thou into the joy of thy lord.**
>
> **Matthew 25:21**

**Being faithful in the small things prepares you to rule over the powers of darkness.** This is an important principle in the kingdom of God. Because David understood this and was faithful in the seemingly insignificant tasks, he went on to become king of the nation. Perhaps you are in this place right now.

David began by first being faithful to tend his father's flocks in an obscure place, not seen by anyone. It did not appear to be an important job in the natural mind's eye. However, I believe God wanted to see if David would first be faithful to tend his earthly father's physical sheep before He would trust David with his heavenly Father's spiritual sheep.

The Lord usually draws you into this kind of service first. When you are in these early stages of your ministry, the enemy tries to whisper in your ear, ''Nobody is giving you enough recognition. You're not doing anything worthwhile.'' Always remember, you can count on the enemy to tempt you to give up when you first start serving and ministering in the Lord's work.

David knew that he was sent to tend the sheep, so he was faithful to do it. Do you know what David was doing when God sent Samuel to anoint him as king? He was tending the sheep. In fact, David's father had to send someone to bring David in from the flocks so Samuel could anoint him (I Samuel 16:1-13).

David was in the will of God tending those flocks. He was right where God wanted him to be. God knew where to find David when it was time to bless him.

It was not always easy for David to be in the will of God. He faced several life-threatening challenges. To protect his flocks, he had to single-handedly fight a bear and a lion; but God helped him overcome.

Do you know what those trials did for David? They prepared him for a greater challenge: his battle against Goliath. What happened after he fought Goliath and won? David's victory in this one battle was the catalyst that brought him into the king's service and family; he then married the king's daughter.

Eventually the event that looked like David's destruction was the very thing that took him to the throne. God was in control of it all.

Are you fighting any "Goliaths" in your life right now? Is a problem gripping your heart? I want you to know that God will turn it around for His glory.

When you are in the will of God, you are going to face some challenges. I wish I could say that you will have no problems or pressures at all. If I had written the Bible that's what I would have put in it; but I want you to hear the truth. It will set you free.

When many Christians are even mildly attacked by the devil, they think God has forsaken them. No! God is preparing them for a destiny.

He is preparing *you* for a destiny. It will be greater than anything that you could ever want or ask for your life; but you need to do it God's way. You need to go where He tells you to go and do what He tells you to do, even if it seems to be an insignificant job like tending sheep. The flock that God has assigned you to tend could be in one of many places:

- A C.A.R.E. home fellowship group
- A classroom
- A nursery — sheep sometimes smell; you might be called upon to change smelly, dirty diapers!

However, when you are faithful in the little things, then God will prepare you for much. Don't say, "When I can sing a solo in the choir, that's when I'll be ministering to the Lord." No! God's kingdom does not work this way. Join the choir; join the orchestra; be a faithful member of the group and then God will prepare you for much.

**And whosoever will be chief among you, let him be your servant....**

**Matthew 20:27**

## Use the Name of Jesus

Paul encouraged the church at Ephesus to walk in Jesus, in the power of the *mighty Name of Jesus*. You, too, have this awesome weapon at your disposal to defeat your enemy. Use it daily. Understand its power.

> The eyes of your understanding being enlightened; that ye may know what is the hope of his calling, and what the riches of the glory of his inheritance in the saints,
>
> And what is the exceeding greatness of his power to us-ward who believe, according to the working of his mighty power,
>
> Which he wrought in Christ, when he raised him from the dead, and set him at his own right hand in the heavenly places,
>
> Far above all principality, and power, and might, and dominion, and every name that is named, not only in this world, but also in that which is to come:
>
> And hath put all things under his feet, and gave him to be the head over all things to the church,
>
> Which is his body, the fulness of him that filleth all in all.
>
> **Ephesians 1:18-23**
>
> Wherefore God also hath highly exalted him, and given him a name which is above every name:
>
> That at the name of Jesus every knee should bow, of things in heaven, and things in earth, and things under the earth;
>
> And that every tongue should confess that Jesus Christ is Lord, to the glory of God the Father.
>
> **Philippians 2:9-11**

The Name of Jesus is above *every* other name you can possibly think of. *Everything* has to bow its knee to the Name of Jesus. That includes sickness, poverty, marriage problems, strife, negative thoughts, drug and alcohol addictions, weight problems, eating disorders, the spirit of religion, and every demon in existence today. In fact, the Name of Jesus is more powerful than Satan himself.

Using legal terms, I could say that Jesus gave His *power of attorney* to you. When you have a power of attorney, you can act in another person's authority. You have *legal* rights to all the possessions that belong to that person.

I have power of attorney to use my husband's name. Soon after we signed the papers for this, Lawrence went on a trip to Canada. We needed a new car at the time, so I decided to see how this worked. (I had never had power of attorney before. I just wanted to make sure it worked, in case an emergency came up later when he was out of town!) So I went out and bought a car. It was a great car!

When Lawrence came home, he said, "I can't believe you bought one of our first brand-new cars while I was out of town."

I said, "You gave me power of attorney." He could not argue with that. My husband is very gracious — I still have power of attorney!

Jesus Christ has given to you *His* power of attorney. You can use His Name; nothing can stand against that Name. Nothing! No enemy! Nothing can stop you! Jesus said:

> **"Behold, I give you the authority to trample on serpents and scorpions, and over all the power of the enemy, and nothing shall by any means hurt you...."**
>
> **Luke 10:19 (NKJV)**

This is for every believer. Have you been worried or plagued by something that is trying to harm you? Maybe it is a fear of death. Start speaking the power of the Name of Jesus against that circumstance. The Lord promises that nothing shall harm you.

On the night I encountered that demonic spirit in my hotel room in Phoenix, the only word I could say at first was, "Jesus." I was so afraid that I could barely breathe. However, as I continued speaking the Name of Jesus, power began to come into my life.

When you speak in the Name of Jesus, the devil is just as powerless against you as he is against Jesus Himself! *In other words, the Name of Jesus empowers you with all the authority that belongs to Jesus Himself!*

## Storm the Gates of Hell through Prayer

Tennyson, the English poet, discovered the secret power of *prayer* in the 1800s. He wrote:

> **More things are wrought by prayer**
> **Than this world dreams of.**
> **Wherefore, let thy voice**
> **Rise like a fountain for me night and day.**

In our church in North Dallas, many women have committed themselves to God and to our church to be dedicated prayer warriors. Why do these women pray? They have found that prayer empowers them to storm the gates of Hell to defeat the enemy. It really works. James 5:16 says:

> **...The effectual fervent prayer of a righteous man availeth much.**

The *Amplified* translation of this verse says that prayer "...makes tremendous power available...." When you pray, you are unleashing the *full power* of God into a situation.

Jesus said that we are to take back *forcefully* the ground the enemy has stolen. *In other words, we are to pray with force to break down the strongholds of the devil.*

> "...From the days of John the Baptist until now the kingdom of heaven suffers violence, and violent men take it by force."
>
> **Matthew 11:12 (NASB)**

Not only are we to pray with force, but we are to pray in faith. *Force plus faith equals victory in your life.*

> "Therefore I say to you, whatever things you ask when you pray, believe that you receive them, and you will have them."
>
> **Mark 11:24 (NKJV)**

You *will* receive whatever you ask when you ask in faith. Don't be afraid of the works of the devil. You have the power through prayer in the Name of Jesus to stop him. You have the force through that Name above all names to storm the gates of Hell and to break the enemy's power over your life. Use it.

Another powerful weapon that is available to every believer is praying in the Holy Spirit or in unknown tongues. *Praying in the Spirit causes the will of God to manifest, even when you do not know how you should pray in a given situation.*

> Likewise the Spirit also helpeth our infirmities: for we know not what we should pray for as we ought: but the Spirit itself maketh intercession for us with groanings which cannot be uttered.
>
> And he that searcheth the hearts knoweth what is the mind of the Spirit, because he maketh intercession for the saints according to the will of God.
>
> **Romans 8:26-27**

Praying in the Spirit strengthens and empowers you with the anointing of God and brings you into victory.

**But ye shall receive power, after that the Holy Ghost is come upon you: and ye shall be witnesses unto me both in Jerusalem, and in all Judaea, and in Samaria, and unto the uttermost part of the earth.**

**Acts 1:8**

**But ye, beloved, building up yourselves on your most holy faith, praying in the Holy Ghost....**

**Jude 1:20**

**And it shall come to pass in that day, that his burden shall be taken away from off thy shoulder, and his yoke from off thy neck, and the yoke shall be destroyed because of the anointing.**

**Isaiah 10:27**

Do you need changes in your life? Do you need a yoke broken off your life? Is there something — that you have not been able to overcome — hindering your walk with God? If so, start praying. Seek God. Allow His powerful anointing to break that stronghold. He can change *any* situation, no matter how hopeless it looks in the natural.

Isaiah 59:19 says, "...When the enemy shall come in like a flood, the Spirit of the Lord shall lift up a standard against him [the enemy]." As you seek the Lord today, I believe you will receive a miracle in your life. That's a promise to you from God.

## Be a Doer of the Word

Merely walking in *obedience* to the Lord — being a *doer* of His Word — is another extremely powerful weapon of spiritual warfare.

In August of 1989, Lawrence and I agreed to go to the Power Team crusade in Phoenix with John and Ruthanne Jacobs, although in the natural realm it did not fit into our schedule. I really thought we didn't have time to go, but the Lord spoke to me, "Go to that conference."

I believe that my obedience to God's will empowered me to overcome the demonic force that came into our hotel room the last night of the conference.

You see, when you are in the will of God, your obedience to the Lord gives you power and authority through Jesus Christ. One reason for this is that when you walk in obedience, you have faith. Faith equals power.

> **Beloved, if our heart does not condemn us, we have confidence toward God.**
>
> **And whatever we ask we receive from Him, because we keep His commandments and do those things that are pleasing in His sight.**
>
> **I John 3:21-22 (NKJV)**

Faith comes when you walk right — walk in the Word — and are a doer of the Word. It empowers you to remain standing during great storms. Are you facing any great storms right now?

> **Whosoever cometh to me, and heareth my sayings, and doeth them, I will shew you to whom he is like:**
>
> **He is like a man which built an house, and digged deep, and laid the foundation on a rock: and when the flood arose, the stream beat vehemently upon that house, and could not shake it: for it was founded upon a rock.**
>
> **But he that heareth, and doeth not, is like a man that without a foundation built an house**

upon the earth; against which the stream did beat vehemently, and immediately it fell; and the ruin of that house was great.

Luke 6:47-49

But be doers of the word, and not hearers only, deceiving yourselves.

For if anyone is a hearer of the word and not a doer, he is like a man observing his natural face in a mirror;

for he observes himself, goes away, and immediately forgets what kind of man he was.

But one who looks intently at the perfect law, the law of liberty, and abides by it, not having become a forgetful hearer but an effectual doer, this man shall be blessed in what he does.

James 1:22-24 (NKJV), 25 (NASB)

Do you need blessings in your home, your job, your finances, or your relationships with others? Here is the place to begin: be a doer of the Word. Stay in His will.

You can hear teaching, after teaching, after teaching on how to stay in the will of God. However, it can often be difficult to know His will for your life. When you sense that the Lord is giving you personal direction regarding His will, how do you know if it is *really* from Him?

One way is to test it against the Word in your heart. Ask yourself, *Is this plan scriptural?* You have to read the Word every day or you will not know. I really mean that. People can tell you what they think of your plan, but you must read the Bible to have the Word in your heart as your standard.

You have to first hide the Word in your heart. Then when you need it, the Holy Spirit will bring it to your remembrance. That is how the Lord gave me the Scriptures in Korea to teach you about spiritual warfare. The Holy Spirit simply reminded me of the Word that I had hidden in my heart years before. Then I began to meditate on these truths and pray for a deeper revelation.

If you need to make an important decision or need guidance, the Lord will tell you what to do. However, it will not help you unless you hear His voice — the *rhema*, or the spoken Word — and do it. Then also do what the *logos* — the written Word — says. Before you know it, you will begin to receive blessings in all you do.

Do you want to win at everything you do? Do you want your marriage to work; do you desire your children to rise up and call you blessed; do you want blessings in every area of your life? I want to show you the key to achieving all of this. You must walk in obedience to the Lord. Let me tell you a true story.

> **So the Lord said to Joshua: "Get up! Why do you lie thus on your face?**
>
> **"Israel has sinned, and they have also transgressed My covenant which I commanded them. For they have even taken some of the accursed things, and have both stolen and deceived; and they have also put it among their own stuff.**
>
> **"Therefore the children of Israel could not stand before their enemies, but turned their backs before their enemies, because they have become doomed to destruction. Neither will I be with you anymore, unless you destroy the accursed from among you.**
>
> **"Get up, sanctify the people, and say, 'Sanctify yourselves for tomorrow, because thus**

says the Lord God of Israel: "'There is an accursed thing in your midst, O Israel; you cannot stand before your enemies until you take away the accursed thing from among you.' ' "

Joshua 7:10-13 (NKJV)

When walking in disobedience to the Lord, you are *assured* of defeat. Why has Satan defeated the church for so long? It is because we are in disobedience; the enemy has been deceiving Christians, saying, "Go ahead, sin. Nobody will know. It's all right. Do your own thing. Talk badly about that person; rip her apart; gossip a little bit." The Body of Christ has been falling into the enemy's trap of disobedience.

What should you do if you find yourself in this situation — if you know that you are not walking right with God in certain areas of your life? Stop and do what the Word says in I John 1:9, repent: "If we confess our sins, he is faithful and just to forgive us our sins, and to cleanse us from all unrighteousness."

It is not very hard. It does not take a long time. Stand at His feet, love Him, and say sincerely, "Lord! It's me again. I'm sorry. I fell into that again. Forgive me. I accept Your forgiveness, and I walk in Your liberty right now."

Whatever you have done — this really is the truth — God can forgive you. (However, of course, we are not to use God's mercy and forgiveness as a license to sin.)

When you repent, you are empowered to become an overcomer in every circumstance you face. You might face some difficult circumstances, and you might not think at first that you can walk through them; but God promises that you *will* be victorious.

**The enemy wants to keep you anemic, weak and ineffective. He knows that when you are obedient and right**

*Overcome by the Power of the Spirit*

**with God, you are a powerful, life-changing force in this world!** Woman of God, you are going to break whatever has chained you up spiritually while reading this book through the power of the Holy Spirit! I really believe that!

- Daniel's obedience took him first to the lion's den, but then to great favor with the king and much success (Daniel 6:1-28).
- Joseph's obedience took him first to the prison cell, but then to the king's palace as second in command over the nation of Egypt (Genesis 39-41).
- Shadrach's, Meshach's, and Abed-nego's obedience first took them to the fiery furnace, but then to prosperity under the direction of the king (Daniel 3:1-30).
- Jesus Christ's obedience first took Him to Calvary and to the tomb, but then to the resurrection and ascension into glory, gaining the redemption of all mankind! (Luke 22-24).

In each case, victory came after a seemingly hopeless situation. God used the terrible circumstances — which could have been stumbling blocks — for His glory. There is hope for *every* situation.

Remember, Jesus came to give you "abundant life" (John 10:10). I have seen temporary defeats become stumbling blocks of destruction in many women's lives; but I have also seen them become stepping stones to success. It all depends upon each woman's attitudes and how she handles the trials.

If you want victory over *your* circumstances, you must be obedient and operate according to the Word:

**Casting down imaginations, and every high thing that exalteth itself against the knowledge of**

**God, and bringing into captivity every thought to the obedience of Christ...**

**II Corinthians 10:5**

Stop each thought that is contrary to the Word *before* it becomes a stronghold in your mind. It is much easier to pluck out a tiny seedling than a huge oak tree. Don't wait until that thought takes root in your mind. Destroy it with the Word. Be obedient to the Lord, then He will turn your trials into stepping stones to success and victory!

# Part IV
# Women: To Arms!

# 10
# Fight until You Win

As a pastor's wife, I have had the opportunity to see many problems in individuals' lives that most people do not ever encounter. I have counselled numerous women in the throes of despair — families ripped apart, destruction, hopelessness. Many of them have faced horrendous struggles.

In every case, when these women drew their strength, power, and courage from God, I have seen them turn mountains of stumbling blocks into stepping stones for success. These problems could have totally devastated their lives if they had seen their troubles through the natural mind's eye. In fact, many of these mountains became the very catalysts that propelled them into their future dreams such as we studied in a previous chapter with David; Daniel; Joseph; Shadrach, Meshach, and Abed-nego; and Jesus.

What are you facing in your life that is really difficult? Maybe the enemy has been trying to knock you out. Maybe he has been beating you and your family. Maybe your emotions have been rocked. Maybe despair has been riveted to your life and you are on the brink of no hope.

Has fear of the future been plaguing you? Maybe you feel totally lonely. Maybe you don't know how you can make it another day because you feel so bad about yourself. Maybe you don't have any hope for your mate or your marriage. I want you to know, there is hope. *There is hope.*

Recently, when my husband and I were on Trinity Broadcasting Network, we were talking about marriage. I told the women in the television audience, "When you accepted Jesus, you truly believed that God could make you a new creation. *Now you need to have that same type of faith about your husband and your family.* You need to believe that the Lord truly can change them. He changed you, didn't He? He has changed me. He can change your husband and your family." Remember, the Bible says:

**The king's heart is in the hand of the Lord, like the rivers of water; He turns it wherever He wishes.**

**Proverbs 21:1 (NKJV)**

The hearts of your husband, son, daughter, mother, father, boss, and friend are in the hand of the Lord. Allow Him to move in their lives.

## Are You Struggling with Being Alone and Single?

I know how hard being single can be. I tried to enjoy the state of singleness, but it was difficult for me. Sometimes, I know it can be very lonely being single, but God was with me when I was single. He is with you, too.

Being single was a time of preparation for me. Without it, I could have never made my marriage successful. I first had to become a whole, complete person. When two whole, complete people marry, they become an extremely strong force. However, too many people who are half together marry others in the same condition. The result is two troubled people, living together who wonder why they have problems in their marriage.

If you are single, develop and learn everything God wants you to learn. *Learn it!* Realize that you are in boot camp; you are in training — even if you are fifty years old.

*Fight until You Win*

Pray, learn, and seek God. If it's the desire of your heart and you are right with God, you will find that mate in God's perfect timing.

I have seen many, many couples find God's mates for them by doing this. Don't give up. Don't let the devil torment your mind. It's time that you stand up and arise and declare, "Stop! No more are you going to steal, kill, and destroy in my life, Devil! I believe that as I delight myself in the Lord, He *WILL* give me the desires of my heart" (Psalm 37:4). Amen — so be it!

## Jesus Has Given You the Victory

Do you remember the story in the beginning of this book about the woman who had a fear of flying? She did not deal with it because she did not realize that an enemy was viciously stealing, killing, and destroying in her life. Because she did not stand up and fight that enemy, he destroyed her life. Don't let this happen to you.

A great man of God once told me a story. He had been praying but fell asleep and had a vision. He was standing in his church sanctuary and saw a demonic host surrounding the building. They were scary — in every size and shape imaginable. They were hideous.

Suddenly this man saw that Jesus was standing in front of him. As the enemy approached Jesus to destroy Him, Jesus took a step back. The man thought, "Wait a minute. I expected You to go forward, Lord. The enemy is coming at us and You are retreating? I don't understand."

As the demons continued their approach, Jesus took another step back. It looked like the Lord was retreating, but then He took another step back and *stepped right into this man of God!* After Jesus stepped into the man, do you know what happened? The man of God started stepping *forward.*

Do you realize that Jesus is inside of you, giving you the power to go forward in battle? It's time for you to stop stepping backward. Remember, He is living inside of you, if you are a born-again believer. Nothing shall harm you. Stand up and shout, for He has given you the victory!

About two years ago a friend of ours had twin boys. The babies were *very* premature, each weighing just a little over one pound. My husband and I were called about 11:00 p.m. and asked to go to the hospital to comfort the couple. (The doctors had said there was very little hope for the babies' survival.)

Outside of a miracle, I knew there was no way these tiny babies could live. I had seen premature babies die many times before; but knowing that God is God and that He is "able to do exceedingly, abundantly more than we could ever ask or think" (Ephesians 3:20), I knew the situation was not hopeless.

After talking a few moments with the couple, we realized that they were believing God for a miracle. Lawrence and I knelt down and began to intercede. As I prayed, I saw a vision: Jesus walked into the room where the babies were and placed His large hand on each child.

At that very moment, peace — *a peace that passes all understanding* — filled me. I suddenly *knew* without a doubt that the babies were going to live! Nothing had changed in the natural realm, but I knew it soon would. I told the parents about my vision and shared that I really believed their babies were going to live.

Today, these little boys are alive and a joy to behold! For months, the hospital staff talked about their miracle of survival.

I will be honest; the parents did face challenge after challenge, but the Lord saw them though it *all*. The parents *refused* to let Satan steal their babies. They couldn't stand on their own strength, but relied on the power of the Lord. It worked! It will work for you, too!

Is there a problem or situation you are facing that seems *hopeless* or *impossible?* There is hope because we serve a miracle-working God. Remember, you have victory in Christ Jesus and in Him alone. It is not by power; it is not by might; but it is by His Spirit (Zechariah 4:6).

The problems and failures in your life don't have to be stumbling blocks. If you let Him, God can turn them around to become the stepping stones to your success and victory. He really can! I believe His Word that says He will work all things together for good for them that love God and are called according to His purposes (Romans 8:28).

Start cleansing your mind with the Word. Romans 12:2 says, ''...Be not conformed to this world: but be ye transformed by the renewing of your mind, that ye may prove what is that good, and acceptable, and perfect, will of God.''

God has a wonderful plan for your life. In fact, He has *the best plan* for your life. Don't listen to the enemy's lie when he says, ''You're wasting your time. You have it too rough. Stop serving God. They have it better in the world.'' Don't be like the Children of Israel who said, ''We should be back in slavery in Egypt where it was better.''

Stay focused on the fact that God has a wonderful plan for your life. Don't let the enemy rob you and stop you from seeing that vision for your life fulfilled.

## Do Not Stop Short of Your Dream

I want to share a powerful story with you that I hope you will remember long after today. It will help you keep everything in perspective while you engage in spiritual warfare. It's a story of a woman who trained most of her life to achieve a dream.

This woman's vision was to swim the English Channel. She had trained for many, many years. Finally the day came when she was to compete in a swimming race across the English Channel. Her lifelong goal, which she had so diligently prepared to accomplish, was about to become a reality!

At the proper time, she eagerly jumped into the water and started swimming, stroke, after stroke, after stroke. Suddenly, a fog came rolling in over the water while she was swimming. Her goal — the other shore — became a bit hazy; now she could only vaguely see it in the distance. However, she continued to swim.

Soon she felt a little tired. Her motivation wore thin. Suddenly the woman found the race much more difficult; the vision of her goal was growing cloudy. It had once been clear. When she had begun the race, she could see her course — her destiny, her dream — but now she could barely see it.

Finally, after the fog had grown heavier, she could no longer see the end at all. Her vision became totally blinded and she stopped swimming — only several feet from the other shore. That woman never realized her goal, because she let her vision become clouded and fogged over. She stopped when she could no longer see the end.

Have you let the enemy or the circumstances of life begin to cloud the vision that you know God has placed into your heart for your life? Have you begun to allow your goal to start dimming? You might be only moments away from reaching your lifelong goal. Don't give up. Keep on working toward your dream.

As a pastor's wife I have seen the enemy destroy many believers by luring them off course just before their breakthroughs. They became caught up in the things of the world right before God was to bring the victory and fulfill the promises they had been waiting for. I am tired of seeing this happen.

I knew a woman who had a God-given desire to sing Gospel music. She had an incredible voice. For years it looked like nothing was happening in her singing career. Then, just as she was about to begin ministering with a large singing group in Nashville, something very tragic happened. On the verge of receiving everything that God had placed in her heart, she was caught in adultery. She lost her entire career right when God was opening that door. (I believe in restoration of dreams; I desire to see her restored and singing unto the Lord again!)

I have seen parents and wives convince their unsaved loved ones to go to church. When these loved ones finally started attending church, I have seen the *parents and wives* become offended and stop going to church because of something petty. Do you know what happened to the children? They fell into drug abuse — just when God had answered the parents' prayers. You see, when the parents were faithfully serving the Lord and walking right with Him, He answered their prayers. They had the power to take the enemy's territory. However, when they broke fellowship with the Lord, Satan had the power to steal it back.

The enemy has stolen too many families that were on the verge of serving God. I am tired of it. I am ready to say,

"No more! No more will Satan have any part of my life and any part of your life."

I believe you are going to see victory today. Remember, you are a woman of power. Right now, I encourage you to cast down anything in your life that is coming against the vision God has given you for your life. Put away any thoughts that you are not worthy or that your God-given dream is not going to happen.

God said in His Word, "Delight yourself in the Lord; And He will give you the desires of your heart" (Psalm 37:4, NASB). Ask yourself these important questions:

- Am I delighting myself in the Lord?
- Is this a godly desire, a God-given dream?
- Have I searched the Bible to be sure this desire agrees with the Scriptures?

If you can honestly answer yes to all of the above questions, then don't let the enemy rob you of those desires in your life. Don't be like the woman who spent nearly her entire life training to achieve her dream, but quit only several feet away from her goal.

I have not written this book and travelled across the country sharing this message because I like to write and speak. I have a mandate from God, and it is for you!

I believe you are going to see chains broken off your life when you apply the principles in this book to your circumstances. It's time for you to step forward to achieve your victory in the Name of Jesus!

Is there an area in your life that the enemy has been buffeting you? Has he been manipulating you or your family with one of the weapons that I shared with you earlier? Take your authority in the Name of Jesus. Stand up in faith and tell him now:

**Satan, I am putting my foot down. I rebuke you in the Name of Jesus Christ. No more am I going to allow you, to steal, kill, and destroy my finances, my family, my marriage, my church, my job, my physical health, or any area of my life. From this day forward, you are powerless to steal, kill, and destroy in my life in the Name of Jesus.**

I want to believe God and pray fervently with you about your needs. Remember, the Word says where two or more agree concerning anything, it shall be done (Matthew 18:19). Let's pray that God will return to you what the enemy has stolen. As we pray, I believe miracles are going to happen in your life.

Write me today so I can stand with you in spiritual warfare:

> Coral Kennedy
> P.O. Box 816062
> Dallas, TX 75381

## "Where Do I Go from Here?"

In closing, let me share with you what you need to do, now that you have nearly finished this book.

*1. Receive God's Personal Word for You!*

First, if you are not a born-again believer in the Lord Jesus Christ, none of the power I have described in this book is available to you. It is only for believers, but the Good News is *you can become a believer.*

Turn to Appendix A right now and I will show you how to dedicate or re-dedicate your life to the Lord so you can receive His power today. Jesus can meet your every need, if you first come to Him!

*2. Declare Your Proclamation of Power.*

Located in Appendix B of this book is the most powerful Proclamation that I know of. As you boldly proclaim your stand in Christ to the devil, you are exercising the tremendous authority and power of God Himself.

When Dick Bernal came to our church last year and taught on spiritual warfare, he brought a Proclamation for our congregation to declare over our region of the city. After the service that night, members of our congregation rode buses to different locations of the devil's strongholds in North Dallas:

- Topless night club, modeling studio, and adult book and video store
- High school
- Two city halls
- Drug and crime headquarters area
- New age and metaphysical center
- Abortion clinic
- Financial center

We broke the devil's power that night over our city in the Name of Jesus. Several members took a bus to a nearby topless night club, modeling studio, and adult book and video store. From the bus, they declared a Proclamation (much like the one in Appendix B) and commanded the powers of darkness over that region to leave in the Name of Jesus.

Not too long after reading this Proclamation, we saw in the newspaper that IRS agents seized this book and video store's assets to help pay $3.4 million in civil taxes owed by the owner. The newspaper described this man as ''a California businessman who owns 250 sexually oriented

*Fight until You Win*

stores across the nation," seven of which are in Dallas; the article cited 13 locations in Texas alone.

The newspaper explained that the topless bar and modeling studio have different owners and therefore are still in business;[1] and the adult book and video store reopened shortly afterward.

However, the city has filed suit against this "adult entertainment" facility, claiming that it violates a city zoning ordinance. The case has been tried, but as of the printing of this book, the judgement has not yet been rendered.

I believe our congregation and all the other praying Christians seriously tormented the demonic forces assigned to that region. This shows you the power we have in the Name of Jesus.

The battle does not end here. Our church is dedicated to binding the powers of darkness over our city, the nation, and the world to set the captives free in Jesus' Name — and that includes YOU!

I am asking you now to turn to Appendix B and declare the Proclamation of Power that you find there, just like our church members did that night. In speaking those words out loud, you will be denouncing the enemy's power in your life, family, church, city, and in the nation.

The enemy is truly trying to steal, kill, and destroy. No one is exempt. However, as a child of God, you do have a more powerful force *with* you than the enemy has *against* you.

It is time for you to storm the gates of Hell. Declare your Proclamation of Power out loud to establish God's

---

[1] Henry Martinez, "IRS Seize...Assets," *Lewisville News,* January 9, 1991, p. 1.

rulership, victory, authority, freedom, and restoration in every area of your life!

- Personal life
- Family
- Church
- City
- Nation

Boldly and forcefully declare your Proclamation to bind the strong man and to deliver the captives — those who are blind and oppressed. Pierce the darkness! Bring down the prince of darkness and the spirits over your region. Remember, every knee shall bow and every tongue confess that Jesus Christ is Lord (Philippians 2:9-11)!

I honestly believe that if you will declare this Proclamation, you will see a breakthrough in your finances, marriage, emotions, children, physical body, and in any area where the devil has been tormenting you!

I have heard countless stories of victory from women — like you — who received their answers after declaring this Proclamation *every day*. Several diet clubs, I am told, are using this as part of their curriculums! There is tremendous power available to you. What are you going to do with it? *Wage war in the heavenlies to gain peace in your life.*

*3. Pray the Word.*

Lastly, let me encourage you to refer daily to the Scriptures in Appendix C. Pray the Word over every area of life each day. In doing this, you will render the devil powerless and strengthen your faith. Remember, faith comes by hearing and hearing by the Word of God (Romans 10:17). Stand on the Word against the lies of the devil each day.

This is your day of victory. I am very excited about this message. God's promises are powerfully working in every area of your life. As you pray the Word, I believe you will see physical infirmities go from you in Jesus' Name. Chains will be broken off your life. Freedom, joy and happiness will replace despair, hopelessness, despondency, and depression. This is a new day for you!

Always remember, God has a wonderful, exciting plan for your future. Don't allow the enemy to steal it. You are a woman of power in Jesus' Name! *When you wage war in the heavenlies, peace will come into your life.* Keep fighting until you win!

# Part V
# Appendixes

# Appendix A
# Receive God's *Personal* Word for You!

This can be your moment to turn your life around. The Lord did not direct me to write this book merely to take up space on a bookshelf. I believe that you have been sovereignly guided. It is not by mistake that you are reading this page right now.

I believe today is *your* day for a breakthrough!

Have feelings of inadequacy or depression plagued you and almost crippled you? Has discouragement racked your life so that you have felt like "throwing in the towel?" Have you started to become a little lukewarm? Have you been hit by a physical illness that has you living in fear of the future?

If you are facing any of these situations, I am here to declare to you a very important fact: if you have given God your life, He has promised you a life of abundance — the best life that you could ever imagine (John 10:10). You do not have to receive these satanic attacks. Pray this right now to your heavenly Father:

> **Father, I thank you that I am Your child through the precious blood of Jesus. Today I renew my commitment to You. Forgive me for any sins that I have committed. I reaffirm that I will**

live my life in Your service. Guide me, Father, in Your perfect will for my life in Jesus' Name. Amen.

## You, Too, Can Receive the Power of God

On the other hand, if you have turned your back on God, destruction is waiting for you. You are walking outside His protection in the devil's territory. You are an easy prey for your enemy who roams about, seeking whom he may devour (I Peter 5:8). Now is the time to get right with God. Today is your day to get on track with God. Pray this simple prayer right now if you are out of His will:

> God, here I am. Take me as I am. Make me what You want me to be. Forgive me for my disobedience to You. Forgive all my sins. I accept Jesus as my Lord and Savior now. Wash me clean through His shed blood. Accept me as Your child — a new babe in Christ. Help me to live my life for You from this day forward in Jesus' Name. Amen.

If you just prayed this prayer and meant it with all your heart, you are now a child of God. Congratulations! You are a born-again Christian. You now have every right described in this book. However, you need the *power* to enforce your rights!

As a Christian, you are entitled to a very powerful gift from God: the *baptism of the Holy Spirit.* Throughout this book I have explained the necessity of using the power of God to defeat your enemy. How do you *receive* this power into your life?

The baptism of the Holy Spirit energizes and charges your spirit with the power of God. Before Jesus ascended to Heaven, He told His followers to wait in Jerusalem until they were endued with power from on high (Luke 24:49).

**But ye shall receive power, after that the Holy Ghost is come upon you: and ye shall be witnesses unto me both in Jerusalem, and in all Judaea, and in Samaria, and unto the uttermost part of the earth.**

**Acts 1:8**

Not only does the Holy Spirit give you power to witness to others of Christ, but power to speak the Word and power to bind and to loose.

**Verily I say unto you, Whatsoever ye shall bind on earth shall be bound in heaven: and whatsoever ye shall loose on earth shall be loosed in heaven.**

**Matthew 18:18**

All the way through the book of Acts, we read of how being filled with the Holy Spirit allowed believers to loose men and women from Satan's bondage, bringing them into the kingdom of God, healing them, and releasing them in the liberty of the Spirit.

The baptism of the Holy Spirit gives you the power you need to carry out God's Word in your life. He teaches you God's ways and His plan for your life. Daily He guides you into all Truth. Jesus said the Holy Spirit, ''…shall teach you all things, and bring all things to your remembrance…'' (John 14:26).

Every believer can receive this baptism, including you. Here's how. First ask God to fill you with His Holy Spirit.

**''Now suppose one of you fathers is asked by his son for a fish; he will not give him a snake instead of a fish, will he?**

**''Or if he is asked for an egg, he will not give him a scorpion, will he?**

**"If you then, being evil, know how to give good gifts to your children, how much more shall your heavenly Father give the Holy Spirit to those who ask Him?"**

**Luke 11:11-13 (NASB)**

Ask God for the gift of the Holy Spirit. Believe that you receive. Then begin to praise and worship God with all your heart. Continue until you sense the sweet presence of the Holy Spirit there with you. When this happens, simply yield in faith to Him and let Him speak through you in a heavenly language just like the disciples did in the book of Acts. This is the baptism of the Holy Spirit. It was real then, and it's just as real today! Remember what God said, "...I am the Lord, I change not..." (Malachi 3:6).

If today you accepted Jesus as your Lord and Savior, re-dedicated your life to Christ, or were baptized with the Holy Spirit, please write me today. My husband and I want to send you some "ammunition" to help you fight the enemy. We want to help you continue to walk in your new freedom and power. Write to:

> Church on the Rock-North
> 1615 West Belt Line Road
> Carrollton, TX 75006

# Appendix B
# Declare Your Proclamation of Power

Hear us, O spirits of darkness! We, the people of God, anointed by the Holy Spirit to preach the Gospel to the poor, to heal the brokenhearted, to proclaim liberty to the captives and to set free those who are bound and oppressed, and to proclaim the acceptable year of the Lord, stand fast and strong and courageous in our calling. We remind you, principalities and powers, that the Holy Scriptures, having absolute authority, declare that we who believe will do even greater works than Jesus. Our Lord's early disciples declared, "Lord, even the demons are subject to us in Your Name." We, too, have been given authority to trample on serpents and scorpions, and over all the power of the enemy, and nothing by any means shall hurt us.

We declare confidently that we are faithful servants of the Most High God with clean hearts before Him. We declare war against you, spirits of darkness, and launch a mighty offensive attack against you this day in the Name of Jesus Christ. We are defended by the armor of the Almighty God: the Girdle of Truth, the Breastplate of Righteousness, the Shoes in Preparation of the Gospel of Peace, the Shield of Faith, and the Helmet of Salvation. Today, we are empowered with the Sword of the Spirit of God, which is His mighty Word.

Listen to us, spirits of darkness. Together in full power and authority, we bind you in the Name of Jesus Christ of Nazareth. You loose your holds from our personal lives this moment. We resist you spirits of idolatry, confusion, and religion. We pull down the strongholds in our personal lives: conflict; hostility; strife; criticism; lukewarmness; temptation; negative thoughts; fear; worry; depression; discouragement; condemnation; poor self-image; addictions to food, alcohol, drugs, cigarettes, and foul habits; and poverty. We break all curses and any prayers prayed against us contrary to the will of God. We forgive and release all people who have harmed us in any way, and speak blessings over their lives this day. We live in service to others, and obedience to God and His Word. We walk in love, joy, and peace. We have the mind of Christ and are empowered with divine health and healing. Through Christ Jesus, we can do all things and we fully expect to accomplish the work and goals He has called us to do. Nothing shall stop us.

We denounce any ties with witchcraft, the occult, and satanic and pagan activities. We submit ourselves to Almighty God and resist all forms of evil.

By the authority of the Name of Jesus Christ, we declare that our homes are filled with peace, protection, provision, and happiness. We claim favor in business wherever we go.

We pull down the strongholds in our church and over our city and nation: arrogance, haughtiness, contention, religion, perversion, mammon, addiction, sorcery, murder, war, fear, anger, greed, death, poverty, infirmity and deception. We command you to come down from your high places! Our Father God has promised us in His holy Word that we will "possess the gates of our enemies."

Your rule and dominion shall be no more! All things were made through Jesus, and without Him nothing was made. In Him was life, and this life was the light of men, and the light shines in the darkness and the darkness does not comprehend, nor overcome it. You are powerless to stop an awakening of righteousness in the hearts of men, women and children in our city and nation. We, the children of Light, washed clean by the blood of the Lamb, penetrate your strongholds of evil and set the captives free this day in the Name of Jesus Christ.

And now, we worship and boldly declare the praises of the Almighty God. We give Him all the glory for freedom, restoration, and victory in every area of our lives.
AMEN!

You may want to change part of this Proclamation to apply more specifically to your own life. I have tried to cover a broad area in this Proclamation so it would apply to many people in many different situations of life.

Write me when you receive the victory, or tell a Christian friend. It will encourage you to believe God for more.

*Additional copies of this* Proclamation of Power *are available on single cards. Now you can easily carry it in your Bible or purse. Wherever you go, you can defeat the powers of darkness and release the mighty power of God into your life and your loved ones' lives. Return the order form located at the back of this book, or write to: Church on the Rock-North, 1615 West Belt Line Road, Carrollton, TX 75006.*

# Appendix C
# Pray the Word of God

Daily pray the Word of God over every important area of your life. Do not let go of God's promises to you. Personalize the Word to each situation by inserting names in each Scripture below. Also, I have left blank space so you can add your own favorite Scriptures in this appendix.

## How to Pray for Your Husband
*Psalm 1:1-3 (NIV)*
Blessed is my husband, _____, who does not walk in the counsel of the wicked, or stand in the way of sinners or sit in the seat of mockers; but _____'s delight is in the law of the Lord and on His law _____ meditates day and night. _____ is like a tree planted by streams of water, which yields its fruit in season and whose leaf does not wither. Whatever _____ _____ does prospers.

*Psalm 32:8, 10 (NIV)*
The Lord will instruct _____ and teach him in the way he should go; He will counsel and watch over my husband. The Lord's unfailing love surrounds _____ who trusts in Him.

*Psalm 90:17 (NIV)*

May the favor of the Lord our God rest upon _____ _____; establish the work of his hands — yes establish the work of his hands.

*Proverbs 2:6*

For the Lord gives _____ wisdom: out of his mouth comes knowledge and understanding.

*Proverbs 21:1*

_____'s heart is in the hand of the Lord, like the rivers of water; He turns it wherever He wishes.

*Isaiah 11:2-3 (NIV)*

The Spirit of the Lord rests upon _____, the Spirit of wisdom and of understanding, the Spirit of counsel and of power, the Spirit of knowledge and of the fear of the Lord; and _____ delights in the fear of the Lord.

*Ephesians 1:17 (NIV)*

I keep asking that the God of our Lord Jesus Christ, the glorious Father, may give _____ the Spirit of wisdom and revelation, so that _____ _____ may know Him better.

*III John 1:2*

I pray that _____ may prosper in all things and be in health, even as his soul prospers.

*Pray the Word of God*

## How to Pray for Your Children

*Psalm 25:4-5 (NIV)*

Show me Your ways, O Lord, teach me Your paths regarding my child(ren), _____. Guide me in Your truth and teach me, for You are God my Savior. My hope is in You all day long.

*Proverbs 10:1 (NIV)*

"...A wise son brings joy to his father, but a foolish son grief to his mother." Let my child(ren), _____ _____, be wise and bring me joy this day.

*Proverbs 20:7 (NIV)*

The righteous man leads a blameless life; blessed is/are his child(ren), _____, after him.

*Proverbs 22:6*

I have trained _____ in the ways of the Lord. When _____ is old, _____ _____ will not depart from it.

*Isaiah 54:13*

My child(ren) shall be taught of the Lord; and great shall be _____'s peace.

*Malachi 4:6*

Lord, in our home, turn my husband's heart toward his child(ren), _____, and the heart(s) of the child(ren) _____ to the father.

*Luke 2:52*

My child(ren), _____, is/are increasing in wisdom and stature, and in favor with God and man.

*Acts 16:31*
I believe in the Lord Jesus. My entire household, including _____, will be saved.


## How to Pray for Healing

*Isaiah 54:17*
No weapon that is formed against _____ shall prosper; and every tongue that shall rise against _____ in judgment I shall condemn. This is the heritage of the servants of the Lord, and our righteousness is of the Lord.

*Jeremiah 33:6*
God will bring _____ health, and will cure _____. He will reveal to _____ the abundance of peace and truth.

*Romans 8:11 (NIV)*
And if the Spirit of Him who raised Jesus from the dead is living in _____, He who raised Christ from the dead also will give life to _____'s mortal body through His Spirit.

*James 4:7*
_____ is submitted to God. _____ resists the devil, and he flees from _____.

*I Peter 2:24*
By His stripes _____ is healed.

*III John 1:2*
I pray that _____ may prosper in all things and be in health, even as _____'s soul prospers.

## How to Pray for Finances

*Deuteronomy 28:8*
The Lord shall command the blessing upon _____'s storehouses, and in all that _____ sets his/her hand to. The Lord shall bless _____ in everything that He has given to _____.

*Proverbs 3:9-10 (AMP)*
_____ honors the Lord with capital from righteous labors, and with the first fruits of all his/her income. _____ will be filled to overflowing with plenty.

*Isaiah 65:24*
And it shall come to pass, that before _____ calls, the Lord will answer; and while _____ is yet speaking, He will hear.

*Philippians 4:6-7 (NIV)*
_____ is not anxious about anything; but in everything, by prayer and petition, with thanksgiving, _____ presents requests to God. The peace of God, which transcends all understanding, will guard _____'s heart and mind in Christ Jesus.

*III John 1:2*
I pray that _____ may prosper in all things and be in health, even as _____'s soul prospers.

## How to Pray for Your Pastor
*Psalm 72:15*
I pray for _____ continually.

*Psalm 90:17 (NIV)*
May the favor of the Lord our God rest upon _____; establish the work of his/her hands — yes establish the work of his/her hands.

*Proverbs 21:1*
_____'s heart is in the hand of the Lord, like the rivers of water; He turns it wherever He wishes.

*Proverbs 24:5-6 (NIV)*
_____ is wise and has great power. _____ is a man/woman of knowledge and increasing strength. For waging war _____ needs guidance, and for victory many advisers. Bring _____ godly counsel.

*Isaiah 11:2-3 (NIV)*

The Spirit of the Lord rests upon _____, the Spirit of wisdom and of understanding, the Spirit of counsel and of power, the Spirit of knowledge and of the fear of the Lord; and _____ delights in the fear of the Lord.

*Ephesians 1:17 (NIV)*

I keep asking that the God of our Lord Jesus Christ, the glorious Father, may give _____ the Spirit of wisdom and revelation, so that _____ _____ may know Him better.

# How to Pray for the Nation

*II Chronicles 7:14*

If God's people, which are called by His Name, shall humble themselves, and pray, and seek His face, and turn from their wicked ways; then will He hear from heaven, and will forgive their sin, and will heal their land, _____.

*Psalm 33:12*

Blessed is the nation, _____, whose God is the Lord; and the people He has chosen for His own inheritance.

*Psalm 101:8 (NIV)*

Every morning the Lord will put to silence all the wicked in the land of _____; He will cut off every evildoer from the city of the Lord.

*Proverbs 10:30 (NIV)*

The righteous will never be uprooted, but the wicked will not remain in the land of _____.

*Proverbs 14:34 (NIV)*

Righteousness exalts the nation of _____, but sin is a disgrace to any people.

*Proverbs 24:23-25 (NIV)*

To show partiality in judging is not good. Whoever says to the guilty, ''You are innocent — ''people will curse him and the nation of _____ will denounce him; but it will go well with those who convict the guilty, and rich blessing will come upon them.

*Ezekiel 11:19-20 (NIV)*

The Lord will give the people of our land, _____ _____, an undivided heart and put a new spirit in her; He will remove from this nation a heart of stone and will give her a heart of flesh. Then _____ _____ will follow His decrees and be careful to keep His laws. The people of _____ will be His people, and He will be their God.

# How to Pray for Lost Loved Ones

*Isaiah 54:17*

No weapon that is formed against _____ shall prosper; and every tongue that shall rise against _____ in judgment I shall condemn.

*Pray the Word of God*

*Acts 16:31*
I believe in the Lord Jesus. My entire household, including _____, will be saved.

## How to Pray for Yourself

*Psalm 119:9-11 (NIV)*
I keep my way pure by living according to the Word. God, I seek You with all my heart. Do not let me stray from Your commands. I have hidden Your Word in my heart, that I might not sin against You.

*Romans 8:1-2, 5-6*
I do not receive condemnation. I am in Christ Jesus, and do not walk after the flesh, but after the Spirit. For the law of the Spirit of life in Christ Jesus has made me free from the law of sin and death. I am not after the flesh. I do not mind the things of the flesh. I am after the Spirit, and therefore mind the things of the Spirit. For to be carnally minded is death; but to be spiritually minded is life and peace. I choose to be spiritually minded. I receive life and peace.

*Romans 8:37*
In all these things I am more than a conqueror through Him who loves me.

*Romans 12:1-2*
I present my body a living sacrifice, holy, acceptable to God, which is my reasonable service. I am not conformed to this world, but I am transformed by the renewing of my mind, that I might prove the good, acceptable, and perfect will of God.

*I Corinthians 13:4-7 (NIV)*

I am patient and kind. I do not envy or boast. Nor am I proud. I am not rude, self-seeking, or easily angered. I keep no record of wrongs. I do not delight in evil, but rejoice with the truth. I always protect others, trust others, and hope for the best. I always persevere in love.

*II Corinthians 10:3-5*

For though I walk in the flesh, I do not war after the flesh. For the weapons of my warfare are not carnal, but mighty through God to the pulling down of strongholds. I cast down imaginations, and every high thing that exalts itself against the knowledge of God. I bring into captivity every thought to the obedience of Christ.

*Philippians 4:8*

Whatsoever things are true, whatsoever things are honest, whatsoever things are just, whatsoever things are pure, whatsoever things are lovely, whatsoever things are of good report; if there be any virtue, and if there be any praise, I think on these things.

*Philippians 4:13*

I can do all things through Christ who strengthens me.

*I John 4:4*

I am a child of God and have overcome the enemy, because greater is He that is in me, than he that is in the world.

# Order Form

☐ Please send _____ *Proclamation of Power* cards. (See Appendix B.) Enclosed is $1.00 per 5½" x 8½" card.

☐ I would like to order _____ sets of Coral Kennedy's 3-tape audio series, *A Woman's Guide to: War in the Heavenlies And Peace in Your Life.* Enclosed is $14.95 per set.

☐ I just dedicated/re-dedicated my life to the Lord. Please send information to me about how to stay in close fellowship with Him and walk in His Word.

☐ I have just received the baptism of the Holy Spirit. Please send "ammunition" to me so I can fight the enemy and continue to walk in the power of the Holy Spirit.

☐ I would like more information about Church on the Rock-North in Dallas, Texas. Please send a free Visitor's Packet.

☐ Please rush this to Coral Kennedy's desk for prayer. I need prayer concerning: _____
_____
_____

☐ This book has helped me receive God's victory in my life regarding: _____
_____

Name_____
Address_____
City _____ State _____ Zip _____
Phone (_____)_____

**Return to: Coral Kennedy • Church on the Rock-North •
P.O. Box 816062 • Dallas, TX 75381**